TONI MORRISON

GARLAND REFERENCE LIBRARY
OF THE HUMANITIES
(VOL. 767)

TONI MORRISON

An Annotated Bibliography

David L. Middleton

GARLAND PUBLISHING, INC. • NEW YORK & LONDON
1987

Library of Congress Cataloging-in-Publication Data

Middleton, David L.
  Toni Morrison : an annotated bibliography.

  (Garland reference library of the humanities ;
vol. 767)
  Includes index.
  1. Morrison, Toni—Bibliography.   I. Title.
II. Series.
Z8595.5.M5 1987 [PS3563.08749]   016.813'54   87-15031
ISBN 0-8240-7970-1 (alk. paper)

Printed on acid-free, 250-year-life paper
Manufactured in the United States of America

For Brian

PHOTO CREDITS

CONTENTS

INTRODUCTION

Toni (Chloe Anthony Wofford) Morrison burst on the literary scene in 1970, and already her fiction has inspired the kind of sustained critical reflection characteristically afforded a major American novelist. The four books she produced within 11 years comprise a substantial body of work measured by any standard, but it must be said that at least in part because of her being black and a woman that fiction has focused a tremendous amount of attention and generated a wide range of critical responses. The sheer quantity of scholarly work done on Morrison is indeed impressive, appearing in small circulation, ethnic magazines and journals, in mainline publications in America and abroad, in collections of essays, and in books, monographs, and even the inevitable dissertations that mark the appropriately weighty presence of an author worthy of the scrutiny of academe.

At age 55, and with a new novel scheduled for release in the fall of 1987 already chosen as a Book of The Month Club main selection, Morrison's productive career is undoubtedly not over. Yet there is now evidence of a critical consensus placing her in the very first rank of feminist novelists, as well as among the more notable of contemporary American authors generally. In Section II of the pages that follow, I have made a special effort to draw attention to writings by Morrison other than her novels. Those non-fiction items included in the bibliography, arranged chronologically so as to glance at the evolution of her thought, afford a unique insight into her view of herself as black and female. Working with the expository aims of a journalist, Morrison is less oblique about her personal and social values than she is when wearing the novelist's mask. The aggressive tone she consistently adopts, the rigor with which she calls time and again for improvement in the situation of black persons in this country, the bleakness with which she views race relations--such are aspects of Morrison's persona that may surprise or even offend readers who have been aware only of her fiction and its rather exclusive focus on the relations within black families and communities.

For certain of the same reasons cited above, interviews with Morrison, arranged chronologically in Section III, have been annotated in unusual detail with the hope of compensating in part for the relative paucity of information about her. Though her methods of fiction writing are frequently nonrepresentational, Morrison's prose is also an eye-on-the-object type that mirrors contemporary reality to a high degree. Thus traditional, historical scholarship which draws upon biography and upon close study of the facts of black culture is potentially illuminating.

Annotations of criticism comprising Sections IV and V of the book fall into two categories: Criticism on General Topics, and Criticism of Particular Works. Within each category, items are arranged alphabetically by the author's last name, or, if unsigned, by the title of the piece. I have examined all selections except for a very few which proved unlocatable and have been cited but left unannotated and unnumbered. Annotations are numbered consecutively throughout the bibliography. No entry is numbered twice, thus cross-referenced entries are indicated by an asterisk (*) and include a note indicating where the user can locate the full citation.

My aim has been to be comprehensive and inclusive as regards criticism. I have examined standard annual bibliographies through 1985, as well as special bibliographies. When annotating individual items which were lengthy and closely reasoned, I have purposefully written full citations. The student researcher, teacher, librarian, or scholar has thus been given not only a condensed sense of the thesis of a piece, but also a sketch of the major points upon which the argument is built. Working through these annotations provides the reader a relatively detailed understanding of the criticism which is available, and having consulted *Toni Morrison: An Annotated Bibliography* one should have no doubt whether follow-up, personal analysis of a particular essay is necessary. I have not, however, evaluated the worth of individual items. The underlying objective has been to afford readers convenient, comprehensive accessibility to critical readings of Toni Morrison's work.

"Criticism" has been taken to mean anything which is analytical, comparative, evaluative, or interpretive in purpose. The only items I omitted were very brief notices of publication in trade magazines, or reviews which were purely descriptive. Even articles from general readership magazines are cited if judged to make an original contribution by setting forward interpretive points unmentioned elsewhere.

I owe a special debt of gratitude to many individuals who assisted me in this undertaking. Particularly supportive through many months of computerized searches and requests for copies of articles were the courteous, helpful reference librarians at Trinity University and at the University of Texas in Austin. In addition, Maria Garcia McWilliams, interlibrary loan officer at Trinity, was tireless with her assistance. The publicity and design departments at Alfred A. Knopf kindly provided me necessary information and photo releases, and Ms. Ronnie Saunders, secretary to Toni Morrison, has been most generous with her time in answering numerous questions and verifying facts. Sincere thanks are also due to the Faculty Development Commission at Trinity University for granting leave time and money which partially funded this project. To my wife Mary I am grateful for the steady encouragement that pushed me toward its completion. Lastly I am grateful to Toni Morrison, currently Schweitzer Professor of the Humanities, College of Humanities and Fine Arts, The University at Albany, State University of New York. Her visit to Trinity's campus in 1984 provided the inspiration to begin what has been a long, richly rewarding task.

Despite everyone's suggestions and meticulous attention to detail, errors and gaps have undoubtedly crept into the book. For such, I alone am responsible.

David Middleton
Trinity University
San Antonio, Tx
1987

LIST OF ABBREVIATIONS

AL	*American Literature*
ArQ	*Arizona Quarterly*
Atl	*Atlantic*
BALF	*Black American Literature Forum*
BlC	*Black Creation*
BlEnt	*Black Enterprise*
BlLit	*Black Literature*
BlSch	*Black Scholar*
BlW	*Black World*
BOT	*Books of the Times*
CentR	*Centennial Review*
CLAJ	*College Language Association Journal*
CLAQ	*Children's Literature Association Quarterly*
ConL	*Contemporary Literature*
Crit	*Critique*
CSM	*Christian Science Monitor*
DAI	*Dissertation Abstracts Index*
ELWIU	*Essays in Literature Western Illinois University*
Ess	*Essence*
EES	*Explorations in Ethnic Studies*
FW	*First World*
GW	*Guardian Weekly*
HarAdv	*Harvard Advocate*
HudR	*Hudson Review*
JEthS	*Journal of Ethnic Studies*
KR	*Kirkus Reviews*
LibJ	*Library Journal*
List	*Listener*
LOS	*Literary Onomastic Studies*
Mac	*Macleans*
MELUS	*Journal of the Society for the Study of Multi-Ethnic Literature of the U.S.*
MMisc	*Midwestern Miscellany*

PART I
WORKS: NOVELS

I. NOVELS

1. *The Bluest Eye.* New York: Holt, Rinehart, & Winston, 1970; London: Chatto & Windus, 1979.

2. *Sula.* New York: Knopf, 1973; London: Allen Lane, 1974.

3. *Song of Solomon.* New York: Knopf, 1977; London: Chatto & Windus, 1978.

4. *Tar Baby.* New York: Knopf, 1981; New York: New American Library, 1981; London: Chatto & Windus, 1981.

PART II
WORKS: OTHER WRITINGS

II.   OTHER WRITINGS

Poetry

5.   "Big Box." *Ms* 8, no. 9 (March, 1980): 57.
      Written collaboratively with her 14 year old son, Slade, the piece
is a verse narrative about three children who get locked away because
they angered the empowered, adult world with the way they exercised
their freedom. Formally, the poem uses loosely structured four line
stanzas with a casual abcb rhyme scheme and a ballad-like 4/3/4/3
rhythm. Including line drawings of the rebellious children causes the
print to be scattered across the page and diminishes the visual
impression of its being a song. A footnote says the "idea," the "beat,"
and "many of the images" are Slade's; Toni handled rhyme and
spelling.
      Main characters include Patty and Mickey and Liza Sue, who,
in asserting themselves as free persons, threaten the adults and so are
put in a big box with three locks on the door. Their parents all visit on
Wednesdays bringing toys of a currently desirable sort, but the fact
remains the kids are imprisoned. That subtle conflict is mirrored by
the tension between the form and the content of the verse, since it is a
bouncy, upbeat structure and an implicitly depressing subject matter
concerning a variety of childhood nightmare fantasy: being locked up
for disobedience. The parents show apparent concern, but when they
believe themselves challenged, they lash out.
      The refrain, like that of many ballads, reinforces the main idea
of the verses, as follows:
      Oh sea gulls scream, and rabbits hop
      And beavers chew trees when they need 'em.
      But Patty and Mickey and Liza Sue--
      Those kids can't handle their freedom.

Drama

      Dreaming Emmett. Unpublished.
      A drama on the life of Emmett Till, the work was commissioned
by the New York State Writers Institute of State University of New
York and performed by the Capitol Repertory Theater of Albany under
the direction of Gilbert Moses. The premier performance was
dedicated to Martin Luther King, Jr., and commemorated the first
federal celebration of his birth. It was co-sponsored by the Capitol
District Humanities Program, University at Albany.

6. *New Orleans*. Unpublished.
    Discussed in the introduction to the American Audio Prose
    Library recordings done with Ms. Morrison, this work is a musical
    comedy about the Navy's closing of Storyville in 1917. See item 28.

Editions

7. *The Black Book*. Compiled by Middleton Harris, with the assistance
    of Morris Levitt, Roger Furman, Ernest Smith. Introduction by Bill
    Cosby. Edited by Toni Morrison. New York: Random House, 1974.
    198 pages of scrapbook-like material related to the history of
    blacks in the United States comprise this valuable miscellany. Besides
    countless pictures and engravings of entertainers, of lynchings and
    burnings, of sports figures and cowboys and whalers, of inventions
    and utensils and handicrafts, besides maps of the Underground
    Railroad to Canada and shots of nameless individuals, the book is also
    the repository for illuminating prose excerpts. Documents pertaining
    to the slave trade have been included, with instructions for the creation
    of voodoo dolls and hexes, for dream analysis and recipes, together
    with many other anecdotal comments about the social and artistic
    culture of black people.
    An eclectic approach is maintained throughout. The aim is to
    provide readers with a wide-ranging cross section of information
    pulled from 300 years of history, its total effect being to afford a fuller
    sense of what it has meant to be black in America.
    Although general acknowledgements are provided for photo
    credits and previously printed material, individual entries are, with
    few exceptions, not cited in such a way that readers can identify their
    source.

Essays/Reviews

1971

8. "To Be a Black Woman." *NYT Mag* 28 March, 1971, Vol. 7, p.8.
    This review article is required reading for anyone trying to get
    clearly in mind what TM believes about women generally and black
    women in particular. Certainly it should be studied carefully as
    background and context for her essay later in 1971 on the black woman
    and women's liberation. See item 10.

The subject at hand is a collection of writings called *To Be a Black Woman* edited by Mel Watkins and Jay David (New York: William Morrow and Company, 1971). TM indicts it scathingly. Her general criticism is that the book does not, as it seems to purpose, dispel illusions about black women, but instead confirms them. Although its subtitle indicates the work is culled from both fiction and nonfiction, TM says the whole thing is fiction, but done with kind words and euphemisms so as to cause to emerge a picture of the black woman as "an oppressed but sexy, sexy but emasculating bitch" (p. 8). Adopting a premise of feminist criticism, Morrison asserts that despite their best intentions the editors are "befuddled " by their subject, probably because they are themselves males and cannot as a result ever truly comprehend the woman as topic. Of the 39 selections in the book, she notes that fewer than 1/3 are by women. In addition to betraying a gender bias, the book includes what she terms racist scholarship by Abram Kardiner and Lionel Ovesey.

Another basic flaw in the work is that although it supposedly sets out to examine and remove stereotypes about black women, it does not critically evaluate widely held myths about black men. TM does not admire the "facile" generalizations of Calvin C. Herndon nor the verse of Fenton Johnson and Francis E.W. Harper. Even some selections which she considers to be of literary merit, she believes have been misused to serve the editors' ends.

Writers included in the collection whose work is so artful or so intelligent that it cannot be anything but effective include Paule Marshall, Don E. Lee, Jean Toomer, and W.E.B. DuBois.

9.   "Good, Bad, Neutral Black." *NYT Mag* 2 May, 1971, Vol.7, p. 3ff.

Looking with an editor's judgemental eye, TM assesses books designed for black children and shows her appreciation for those which evidence high quality writing making them "human" in the broadest sense and not narrowly racial. That which is truly good becomes universal: "Like so much that is meant for black folks, like so much that black people do for themselves, it ends up in the marrow of the culture at large" (p. 3).

As a group, she finds the biographies commendable, and she holds up Charlamae Rollins, *Black Troubadour* (Langston Hughes) as particularly noteworthy. In the category of folklore, she extols Eliz S. Helfman, *The Bushmen and Their Stories,* and Mesfin Habte-Marian, *The Rich Man and The Singer: Folktales From Ethiopia,* and Paul Glass, *Songs and Stories of Afro-Americans.* Her greatest enthusiasm is reserved for Tony Cade Bambara's *Tales and Stories For Black Folks.*

Perhaps it is at this formative level, in the minds of the children, that genuine, positive social change can take place. Indeed, that change may already be at work in literature, because "unless there is still some confusion about being both black and human, the hubub about black literature is cretinous" (p. 3).

10. "What the Black Woman Thinks About Women's Lib." *NYT Mag* 22 August, 1971, Vol. 6, p. 14ff.

Simply put, the thesis of this essay is that black women distrust women's lib and have not become deeply involved in it because they do not believe it can serve their particular ends.

TM opens by wryly affirming the value of the word "women," as does the movement. During segregation times, Morrison notes, signs for female restrooms were subtly revealing: those for blacks were marked "women," and those for whites "ladies." The latter she takes to mean someone basically weak and ineffectual, the former someone tough, capable, and immodest in the positive sense (p. 15).

One reason for the suspicion black women feel for the movement is their conviction that, at its deepest level, women's lib is a struggle between white women and white men, i.e., a class conflict concerning power. Consequently women are not allies across racial lines; the problems facing the black woman and those facing the white woman are simply too different. At present black women are engaged in a basic economic struggle merely to be heads of households and to get themselves into the workforce--not into law school or medical school.

TM believes the "archetypes" of black women have been created largely by males, but even so (and there is a limitation implied) such archetypes have about them the "smell" of truth. Nefertiti has become for many black women a symbol of beauty, but TM cautions them that the symbol can be insidiously misleading (see item 8 above). Black women are beautiful without having long necks, and more importantly, she says, is their beautiful capacity to endure. She mentions Sapphire as an "archetype" of the nagging wife but notes the latter had a husband who did precisely and merely what he wanted to do. Geraldine, the character brought to life by Flip Wilson, comes to stand for certain "archetypical" characteristics of black women-- humorously defined--because she/he is so stridently defensive, cunning, sexy, egocentric, and a transvestite to boot. However each of those qualities, TM insists, can be turned so that its other side is recognizable as an asset. For defensive, read "survivalist;" for cunning, "clever;" for sexy, "natural acceptance of her sexuality;" for egocentric, "individualistic;" for transvestite, "male strength." Thus that which is presented in comedy as a weakness and a source of humor is at the same time a strength and a source of pride.

The freedom which white women want and now struggle for through the women's lib movement, the black woman has always had. In the latter's case that freedom went under the name of "responsibility" though, and it was forced on her. Behind the distrust black women feel for the movement lies a deep and basic conviction

13

on their part that they are superior to white women. Black women have no respect for white women of the sort that would grow out of "awe at their accomplishments" (p. 64) because white women, for the most part, have no record of accomplishment. They have turned their children over to the black woman to nurse and to raise, and the latter did that job with dignity and love, sometimes even at the expense of her own children. And out of that lack of respect, that feeling of superiority, springs a tremendous anger in black women when black men marry white women. They cannot understand why a man would want to ally himself with an individual who is not worthy of respect. In fact, TM says, black women in truth do womankind a great disservice when they become domestics or take over the burdens of childcare and in so doing provide the means for white women to "escape the responsibilities of womanhood" (p. 64).

One final reason why black women have not affirmed the women's lib movement is that black men are "formidably opposed" to involvement of black women in it.

1973

11. "Cooking Out." *NYTBR* 10 June, 1973, pp. 4, 16.
Cooking a down home, lavish, picnic banquet by a lake becomes the occasion for such fellowship that it is a kind of family communion. The arrival of Uncle Green, ancient and venerable ancestor, is the reason for a reunion and old fashioned cookout.

Uncle Green carries with him the stories, the tang of the old language, the spirit that represents the collective experience of "the tribe" before its members migrated North out of Alabama. In multiple and mysterious ways, this honored elder draws the family together. He inspires possessive jealousy among the women in different branches of the bloodline; he renews the males' sense of their manhood. Like the legendary Solomon of TM's third novel, Uncle Green had married a girl named Sing and fathered seven sons, and now he passes on to the youngsters bits of folk wisdom.

The article is also a means of introducing seven books on outdoor cooking, which the reader will find listed at the end.

1974

12. "Behind the Making of The Black Book." *BIW* 23 (February, 1974): 86-90.
TM identifies the motives which lay back of her deeply felt need to produce *The Black Book*. Disturbed by what she considered to be a "quality of the mystic and the reactionary in our new version of

history" (p. 87), TM determined to correct that currently fashionable and, in her view, unhistorical, black sense of self. She believes in the reality and the efficacy of enduring myths, and consequently is incensed by a myopic tendency in the contemporary black movement merely to defend new ideas or--and this impulse is more regrettable-- to destroy old ones, rather than affirming the truth of the history which has always been theirs.

The result of TM's convictions is this book, 18 months in the making, a collection of data which attests to "Black life as lived" (p. 89), 208 pages of black reality (newspaper articles, songs, pictures, recipes) which *in toto* evidence the presence of underlying myths. This article is her editorial testament to the book's genesis and its significance.

13.   "Rediscovering Black History." *NYT Mag* 11 August, 1974, Vol. 7, p. 14ff.

This essay was written on the occasion of the publication of *The Black Book*. It was designed to clarify the sense in which *TBB* is a unique manifesto. TM talks about the conception and purpose of the phrase, "Black is beautiful," which she says was coined to offset color values so long affirmed by white culture. Though she considers the new phrase necessary, she calls it "irrelevant" and stirs the ire of its creator, William Allen, who responds to her in a letter in the *NYT Magazine*, September 29, 1974, Vol. 7, p.14. But TM did not mean that the phrase was inconsequential or trivial. She had in mind the idea that now, more than a decade after the fact, one can see its danger: its implicit emphasis on looks and image. Blacks need to value intelligence, resiliance, skill, tenacity, irony, and spiritual health. Yet the political expediency of the civil rights movement necessarily caused the movement to ignore aspects of black history and culture that now can be seen to be valuable. As American life moved toward the close of the 70's, TM felt it was time to take another look at black history from a slightly different angle. The point now was to "rescue those qualities of resistance, excellence, and integrity that were so much a part of our past and so useful to us....to bear witness to the quality and variety of black life"(p. 14).

Thus in *TBB* TM aimed to present black life and thought so as to distinguish it, and at the same time she wanted to add to that distinctiveness those qualities that unite black life "with all of mankind" (p. 16). Her research made her despise the consistent effort through white history to insist on the ugliness of their "property" (the slaves). TM wonders aloud whether the repugnance some people felt for what was being done in Vietnam would have been evident if the fighting had been going on in an African country where the people were not considered as beautiful as the Vietnamese. She uses much of her column to blister whites for their inclination to have a double standard for viewing history. Out of the pain and oppression of their past, the blacks managed not only to endure but also to prevail and to sustain a noteworthy culture which *TBB* attempts to acknowledge. What made such endurance possible is a tremendous "complicated psychic power one had to exercise to resist devastation" (p.18). Here again one notes TM's marvelous ability to avoid stereotypes and to see with clarity into the unique and compelling corners of the national character.

In *TBB* she points to many kinds of historical facts (the patent for the overshoe; development of the telephone, eggbeater, and cornharvester, etc.) that provide a basis for black pride and a sharp, new sense of accomplishment about their considerable part in shaping American history.

1975

14.   "Reading." *Mademoiselle* 81 (May, 1975): 14.
       The impulse to tell others about a deeply meaningful reading experience caused TM to reflect on her own earlier encounters with impressive novels by Kafka, Auerbach and Camera Laye, but the passion those works had evoked upon first encounter, though recollectable, was gone. Morrison's work as an editor brings scores of manuscripts to her attention. Usually the experience of reading them involves making critical judgements; notably missing is the sense of wonder and delight that makes one a "hungry reader and not a professional one" (p. 14).
       Reading Gayl Jones' manuscript version of *Corregidora* reawakened the old hunger. Jones has rethought and retold the story of black women in radically new terms. The female requirement to "make generations" is presented "as an active, even violent political act" (p. 14). Relations between black men and women are stripped to their combative essence, and Ursa Corregidora as a result becomes a seminal figure who must nag unforgettably the consciousness of readers and writers alike. In TM's editorial and personal opinion, "No novel about any black woman could ever be the same after this" (p. 14).

1976

15.   "A Slow Walk of Trees (As Grandmother Would Say), Hopeless (As Grandfather Would Say)." *NYT Mag* 4 July, 1976, Vol. 7, p. 104ff.
       This illuminating article includes, besides pictures of the author and her family, an overview of the experience of three generations of blacks in the U.S. TM comments on inequities and reforms that have

been made in race relations, and she identifies changes in the attitudes of blacks.

So personally revealing is this piece that it is subsequently cited by others when they allude to major, formative influences in TM's background: her father's hostility toward whites; his throwing a white man down the stairs of their home and tossing a tricycle down after him; the more optimistic sense in her mother that there are "possibilities" in life; the mother's going to make rent payments and always dealing reasonably with folks; the father's single-minded commitment to a work ethic, and his asking the children, even as they grew into adulthood and came home for holiday visits, "Where are you working?"

Such influences give TM deep roots in Ohio and in the sense of community. She notes that she suffers from "racial vertigo that can be cured only by taking what one needs from one's ancestors" (p. 152).

Running through the article is a hard edge of disappointment at the discouraging lack of positive change in the situation of blacks. The metaphor she uses for this ponderous, almost imperceptible movement is "the slow walk of trees." She applauds those economic strides which afford some people independence, and considers progressive the fact that Haitians have arranged for one mass to be in French (their own language), plus the fact that they own stores and community centers (an economic base). She feels that affirmative action programs have been, if not downright lies, at least deceptive, because minority persons in offices and businesses are in truth no better off than those on the streets. Racist reality still prevails.

Thus she applauds the black judges who give "appropriate" punishments as vs. harsh ones; black individuals who move back to the South and buy land there; black business persons who create an economic base. As a group, the blacks whom TM truly admires are those for whom work is real and meaningful; those who refuse to compromise and imitate; those who clarify the past. Specific individuals such as Ben Chavis, Robert Moses (activist), Sterling Brown (poet), Richard Pryor, Muhammed Ali, and Angela Davis among others less well known are cited as outstanding models.

In the end, she draws some hope from the attitude of the new generation of blacks, a generation who have no inclination to apologize, but who feel naturally that they belong.

1979

16. "The Lesson of Cinderella's Stepsisters." *Ms* 8, no. 3 (September, 1979): 41-42.

Returning to familiar subject matter--the folk tale of Cinderella--TM adapts the tale to a strikingly original context. The essay is a modified version of the commencement address given at Barnard

College in May, 1979, in which she looks beneath the surface of the tale at its deep structural meaning. First she ponders the psychological effects which must shape the stepsisters as they grow up continually faced with the model of a mother who enslaves another girl. "Cinderella," she says, if we want to know the truth, is a story about a "household--a world, if you please--of women gathered together in order to abuse another woman" (p. 41). Seen in this light, that antiquated narrative actually concerns a contemporary matter: the problem of feminine power directed at another woman and usually wielded in what is called a "masculine" manner (p.42). TM pleads with the graduates, destined to be women with power, not to abuse that power. Women must not do violence to each other; they must actively resist such violence. Mothers who abuse their children, women who set fire to buses, women who stop promotions of other women, women in social agencies who humiliate clients--all such potentially damaging situations must be resisted by powerful women such as the Barnard graduates. TM asks that the graduates give attention to their "nurturing sensibilities" (p.42). Nothing really worthwhile is "safe" or ever was, but "in pursuing your highest ambitions, don't let your personal safety diminish the safety of your stepsister" (p. 42).

1981

17. "City Limits, Village Values: Concepts of the Neighborhood in Black Fiction." *Literature and The Urban Experience.* Edited by Michael C. Jaye and Ann Chalmers Watts. New Brunswick, N.J.: Rutgers University Press, 1981), pp.35-43.

An important black novelist such as James Baldwin is prevented from praising the value of post-industrial western cities because although he and countless other blacks live in such cities, they are dispossessed, disenfranchised even there. In deploring the urban, the black writer reinforces a major anti-urban sentiment in the national literature of this country. But unlike the mainstream author, the black artist does not consequently affirm the rural; rather he celebrates community values (village values) of the sort that might be thought of as tribal. Either lonely isolation or defiance of village law is considered an outrage by the black writer, although customarily those attitudes are viewed by the mainstream author as heroic, and the central figure in black city fiction yearns not for singularity but for his/her missing ancestor. In the country or village the black character finds not privacy nor nature nor serenity, but rather the opportunity to touch the all important ancestor.

Both recent black fiction (by Toni Cade Bambara, Henry Dumas, R. Fischer, Leon Forrest, Paule Marshall, James Alan McPherson, Albert Murray) and more established examples of prose

(Jean Toomer) need to be examined from the perspective of the role and function of the ancestor in it. When characters make that essential connection, they achieve a kind of wisdom which values racial memory over individual fulfillment. When they do not so connect, they cannot thrive, and then devastation takes place. The true ancestor is frequently a social or secret outlaw whose enduring wish is to go home to the village. So it is that among black writers the city is a sharply limited concept, while the village remains a place of boundless value.

1984

18. "Memory, Creation, and Writing." *Thought* 59 (December, 1984): 385-90.

Here TM clarifies her ideas about the role of memory in the creative process, and about her dual responsibility to her craft and her audience. She opens with this quote from Norwegian painter Edvard Munch: "It is not enough for a work of art to have ordered lines and planes. If a stone is tossed at a group of children, they hasten to scatter. A regrouping, an action, has been accomplished. This is composition. This regrouping, presented by means of color, lines, and planes, is an artistic and painterly motif." The quote addresses an aspect of the fiction writer's creative process which TM believes is at the center of creativity: the connection between a specific item in one's memory and the "entire galaxy of feeling and impression" (p. 385) which surround and attach to that buried item. Memory, for Morrison, is clearly distinguishable from the way things really were. Memory is a conscious act of the self as the writer struggles to recapture the essence of a character like Hannah Peace. Neither the mere concreteness of her name nor the peculiar tint of her skin explains Sula's singularity, so much as the way people "pronounced her name" (p.386), as well as the aura--"an absence of hostility"-- which she gave off. Thus, recollected pieces of experience stimulate the process, while associating the pieces into "a part" becomes the business of creation.

TM relies heavily on memory and creative invention to mystify her work as art and to prevent its "descending into sociology" (p. 386) which a typical criticism of black literature accuses authors of doing too often. For her, the central preoccupation of *Sula* is the mysterious, recollected and invented notion of "having-been-easily-forgiven." It is not the concrete, sociological fact of being black. More specifically, since the novel is about friendship among black women, TM set out to discover "what there is to be forgiven among women" and what "the nature and quality" of such forgivenness is.

Morrison's authorial aim is to engage readers and to disturb them. Doing so means upsetting their coolly objective viewing of fictional data. Traditional tales or folklore help with that aim because they can discompose one's typically literate reading experience and make one respond "as an illiterate or preliterate reader would" (p.387) when alone with his own imagination. To this end, TM adapts the Hansel and Gretel story to mark Milkman's confusion and "cultural ignorance" when he is about to meet Circe, "the oldest Black woman in the world, the mother of mothers..." (p.387). Similarly, she uses a reference to Hagar's bed as "Goldilocks' choice" to communicate Hagar's being a housebreaker and her emotional selfishness (p. 387).

As a black writer, TM's responsibility can never be merely to represent the world mimetically. That is too patronizing because the reality she must confront is "unlike that received reality of the West" (p.388). She must use discredited information (lore, gossip, magic) derived from discredited people. And she must use the presentational characteristics of Afro-Americans: antiphony, the group nature of art, its functionality, its improvisational nature, its relationship to audience performance, the critical voice which upholds tradition and communal values and which also provides occasion for an individual to transcend and/or defy group restrictions (p. 389).

TM has never intended to try to solve social problems; her fiction examines and clarifies them. She illustrates the working of her creative process by noting the many "pieces" of recollection about the tar baby which she gathered, and how she connected them with a guiding motif having to do with "ahistorical and historical earth." Then she identifies seven steps which she took to shape her motif and give it narrative structure, beginning with the rather obvious fact that a character's coming out of the sea marks the opening and closing of the book. She concludes by revealing that her latest novel works toward the revelation of multiple human mysteries: various secrets concealed within characters, plus the suggestion "that just as we watch other life, other life watches us" (p.390).

PART III
INTERVIEWS

1974

19.   "Conversation with Alice Childress and Toni Morrison." *BIC*
       (Annual 1974-75): 90-92.
           Both authors proclaim that art is indeed political and artists
       politicians.What turns art into mere rhetoric is not its insistence on
       bearing witness, but its being poorly done. Both also agree that artists
       and critics serve radically different functions. The good critic,
       according to TM, talks about the work, not about himself, and can be
       enlightening to the writer as well as to readers.
           One must beware, though, of the vested, economic interest the
       critic has in the survival of art. Black writers in particular must realize
       that only blacks can set the criteria for criticism of black art. Such
       criteria must not be dishonest nor self congratulatory nor patronizing.
           In literature there is such a thing as a black women's
       consciousness which is identifiably distinct from a black man's
       consciousness. Neither, however, is better than the other.
           Reflecting on trends in writing in the 70's, TM says black
       writers seem to be focusing on a different concept of evil--the theme
       that preoccupied her in *Sula*. There the characters never tried to
       annihilate Sula because she was evil; unlike white folks, blacks accept
       evil and try to protect themselves from it (p.92). More importantly, all
       black writers have been writing about not being free--the theme ever
       present in their literature.

20.   Gilliam, Dorothy. "The Black Book How It Was." *WashP* 6 March,
       1974, p. B 1.
           Interviewed at the Sheraton-Park Hotel, TM talked frankly about
       her reasons for editing *The Black Book*. She was influenced
       negatively by the misconceived values of persons who recommend
       that blacks "off" their mothers, and who simultaneously idolize
       pimps, whom TM considers failed men. She was influenced
       positively by her conviction that black history was more subtle, more
       admirable, and more whole than one might think who viewed that
       history in a narrow political sense and thus saw it as consisting simply
       of slavery and the 1960's.
           With major contributions from Middleton A. (Spike) Harris,
       Roger Furman, and Ernest Smith, TM gathered memorabilia in
       scrapbook fashion representing 300 years of folk history designed for
       a specific public: the black masses.

1977

21. Stepto, Robert B. "Intimate Things in Place: A Conversation with Toni Morrison." *Chant of Saints, A Gathering of Afro-American Literature, Art & Scholarship.* Edited by Michael S. Harper and Robert B. Stepto. *Massachusetts Review.* 18 (1977): 473-489.

The sense of detail, of feeling, of moods of a place (whether community or particular room) is strong in all of TM's fiction, but uniquely so in *Sula* where the neighborhood becomes like another character. Medallion, Ohio, is limiting, life-giving, meddlesome, and supportive of its folks, and though vividly concrete, it is not actual but was created out of reminiscences of TM's mother based on life in the hills of Pittsburgh.

Sula was a problem in characterization because she was to be the sort of woman who could be used by other people as "the classic type of evil force" (p. 475). Nel, on the other hand, was to be the prototypical salt of the earth type. Each contains elements of the other, such as the deeply hidden desire in Nel--the law-abiding representative of community life par excellence--for the life of abandon, matched by the equally deep desire in Sula for love as possession. Sula is really outside laws, yet she is a model of self-examination, and because of her singularity she has trouble making connections with other people except Nel and Ajax. The pity is she loses them both in the process of learning and applying what she learned from Nel about a classic ideal of the community: love as possession.

Eva and Hannah Peace are intended to be provocative characters who engage and disturb readers. Sula never in her impulsive life does anything as bad as does Eva in assuming a godlike control and killing her hopelessly drug-addicted son. Sula's mother, Hannah, TM's favorite character in the book, was morally "slack" and at the same time comprehensible to the neighborhood and not threatening like Sula. The terror Sula holds for the community is that her sensibilities are not informed by it, so she could quite casually commit an outrage such as putting Eva in an old folks' home.

TM rejects the suggestion that her female characters are emasculating of black men. She parries by asserting it is a truism of history that white men did that demeaning. Black women have always borne enormous responsibilities (now called "freedoms") which necessarily forced them into decision making. As strong as Sula is, though, she is no threat to Ajax because he is himself a whole person who can love and value her without being intimidated.

A shift in thematic concern can be traced through TM's subject matter: black girlhood (*TBE*) becomes black womanhood (*Sula*) which becomes black manhood (*SOS*, referred to by its working title at the time, *Milkman Dead*). As was her pattern in the first two novels, Morrison uses complementary characters in *SOS*, which looks at bonding between two men. Her control of voice in *TBE* was admittedly less than successful, in that she was forced to use a combination of her own voice and the character's. Her fondness for balanced kinds of characters shows up in Shadrack's manic desire for order which is set against Sula's inclination to de-center life. And Soaphead Church (*TBE*) complements with his eccentricism the deep yearning for conformity to white standards of beauty which motivate and destroy Pecola Breedlove.

Teaching, TM admits, probably would get in the way of her writing if it were full-time, because the former demands a critical and self-conscious stance that is foreign to her creative process. Yet her work as a Random House editor is not intrusive and she enjoyed the one class in "Black Women and Their Fiction" which she taught this year, because it offered her an opportunity to go into uncharted waters as regards both fiction and criticism of it. She was intrigued by how black women looked at the stereotypes of black women, how political or apolitical the works by black women were, and how--on a deep structure level--the woman writer really feels about herself.

For black men, no theme is more absorbing than the Ulysses theme. Hence there is a sense of movement about her male figures-- the leaving home. It is motivated by curiosity and leads to self-knowledge as well as to tremendous sociological failings: they are constantly taking off. Some of that is present in Sula; in significant ways, she is quite masculine: adventuresome, self-confident, daring, unafraid--on the edge of or outside the limits of the community. Tracing such a theme through a number of books or through the lives of black artists is what contemporary criticism of black writing should do. Intelligently accomplished, such tracing would identify what is unique to the literature.

Now that it's no longer so fashionable to be "a black writer," authors can go home and get down to serious work. The change is healthy. There is interest in and a vitality about black subjects, and authors should not be discouraged: somewhere there is bound to be an editor or publisher who will understand and respect new black writing on its own terms.

22. Watkins, Mel. "Talk With Toni Morrison." *NYT Mag* 11 September, 1977, Vol. 7, p. 48ff.

Watkins finds TM in her office surrounded by both the books she edited for Knopf, such as the oversize facsimile edition of Muhammed Ali's *The Greatest*, and also her own novels. She sold the serial rights to *SOS* to *Redbook* and it also became the first novel by a black author since Richard Wright's *Native Son* to be chosen Book of The Month Club main selection.

Her working method, she says, is to write in the evenings, which she protects scrupulously by not getting into the social whirl. Typically she does her thinking on the train to work and gestates her ideas while doing dishes, so that when she sits down to paper, she is capable of getting into the writing fairly quickly. Sometimes, though, she will work every day for three or four months, and then do nothing for another three. So there is no definite "routine."

As a matter of approach, TM looks for the "right metaphor" for a scene. For example when at work on *SOS* she had to create a scene that showed Milkman was in a small town, in the country, and thus placed quite differently from the way he had been at home. When she finally decided to write around the image that the women walked down the street "with nothing in their hands" (p.48) the rest of the chapter followed.

She tells of beginning her writing while teaching at Howard University in 1962. A group of about 10 persons got together once a month, each time bringing something to read. One day she took the story of a black girl who wanted blue eyes, and the others in the group liked it. In 1964 she left Howard and went with her family to Europe for the summer. When she returned, her husband did not. She was unhappy, lonely in her job at Syracuse, and so she began work on that story again. In time, writing became a way to "order my experience" (p. 48). She has tried always to focus on language, because, "It's always seemed to me that black people's grace has been with what they do with language" (p. 48).

Her concerns in fiction appear to be widening. The first two novels "focused on the insulated, parochial world of black women" (p. 50). Then in *SOS* she became interested in men "almost as a species" and that interest forced her "to loosen up" (p. 50). She had to become more expansive, to get her action outside of houses, which are the peculiar domain of women. Women, she insists, live in houses, but "men don't live in those houses. They really don't" (p. 50).

Consistently her work has revealed her interest in folklore and magic: "Black people believe in magic" (p. 50). "That's why flying is the central metaphor in *Song*--the literal taking off and flying into the air which is everybody's dream" (p. 50). Somewhat more in the vein of folklore, she has used the African sense of "whirling dervishes and getting out of one's skin, but also in the majestic sense of a man who goes too far" (p. 50). The word "man" is used judiciously, because she believes that it tends to be a male thing "to soar" to take off, to split, and "the price is the children" (p. 50). In *SOS* "all the men have left someone, and it is the children who remember it, sing about it, mythologize it, make it a part of their family history" (p. 50).

TM does not admit to being influenced in any specific ways by other writers such as Gabriel Garcia Marquez, but instead says she is touched and perhaps shaped in broadly inclusive ways by all that she reads.

The story of the tar baby she says always "terrified" her. It is a unique combination of black folklore as history, because it is both a prophecy and a reflection of the past. And perhaps more surprisingly, TM says the tar baby story in the original is a love story. In it the tar baby is the black woman and the rabbit the black man, powerless, clever, and needing to outwit the master. The rabbit is determined to live in the briar patch, even though he has the option to live with her, securely, without magic. "Will she go into the briar patch with him?" the author asks rhetorically. And she leaves the interviewer with the suggestion that the question expresses what her new novel is about.

1978

23. Bakerman, Jane. "The Seams Can't Show: An Interview With Toni Morrison." *BALF* 12 (1978): 56-60.

TM talks briefly about her children, Ford (Dino) and Slade, born in 1961 and 1965 respectively. Here, as in other interviews, she notes that she begins her writing anywhere she has a scene in mind, or even "a feeling, the language, the metaphor. . . . I do those and they may appear at any point in the book" (p.57). In *Sula*, for example, she began with Shadrack. One scene that had to be changed a great deal involves Nel's discovery of her husband, Jude, making love with Sula, and her going into the bathroom to think. Originally the scene was done in prose that was "absolutely beautiful, purely distilled pain" (p. 58), but TM came to realize that such a style was inconsistent with the character, and so it had to be totally revised in terms of Nel's own images, her words.

The influence of myth in TM's work is pervasive. Myths are, for her, the "way that human beings organize their human knowledge--fairy tales, myths. All narration. And that's why the novel is so important" (p. 58). Fiction becomes a way of ordering experience and a way of telling it so that others may participate. TM used smaller kinds of details, such as the plague of robins, in *Sula* to mark a "distortion, something out of kilter in nature" (p.58) evident in Sula's return to the Bottom.

She likes to use first person narrative when assuming a character, as is clear in the 1984 interview in *Black Women Writers* (see item 31 below) when she talks about the importance of the autobiographical form with its stress on the singularity of experience. But when that point of view becomes too much of a burden, she uses a combination of both first person and third.

In this piece appears one of the author's rare admissions that her audience are not particularly black readers nor white ones, but those who will understand (p.59). And she comments on the structural and thematic inclination she has to use complementary characters, in *Sula* the carefully matched pair, Sula and Nel. Those women are "two sides to one personality, 'if they were one woman, they would be complete' " (p. 60).

1979

24. Dowling, Colette. "The Song of Toni Morrison." *NYT Mag* 20
     May, 1979, Vol. 6, p. 40ff.

The article opens with a description of TM talking to an audience
at Sarah Lawrence University and there articulating one of her
convictions that, "what is curious to me. . . is that bestial treatment of
human beings never produces a race of beasts" (p. 40).

When *SOS* was published by Knopf, it was also sold to New
American Library "for a reputable $315,000" (p. 41). There it became
a paperback bestseller, with 570,000 copies in print, and translation
rights sold in 11 countries.

When she went to Howard University, Chloe Wofford decided
to change her name to Toni, ostensibly because people there had a
hard time pronouncing it (p. 42).   Another turning point in her life
occurred at Howard, because it was while she was on tour with the
Howard University players that she learned, as a result of incidents
left undiscussed, "the iniquitous loss of family land to whites" (p.42).

She is from a family of four children; her father, George
Wofford, was a shipyard worker and held down other jobs as well.
He valued work, had a tremendous amount of anger in him, and told
the very best of ghost stories. Her mother, Rahmah, bears a name
that was "picked blind" from the Bible.

TM herself often does little "acts" in her conversation. She will
"get down" and become colloquial, sucking on her teeth, and then
poking her finger into her scalp and scratching. All this is consistent
with the fact that she hides herself "about 60% of the time. . . . I teach
my children that there is a part of yourself you keep from white
people--always" (p. 42).

While she was teaching at Howard University, she met and
married a Jamaican architect, Harold Morrison. In the summer of
1964, they went to Europe, but when she returned, it was alone. She
went to her parents' home with two young children, and year and a
half later took a job with a Syracuse textbook company, a subsidiary
of Random House. She hoped by so doing to be able to have some
effect on the textbooks that America reads, but she soon was working
full time in the trade division. While living in Syracuse, she says that
three noteworthy events occurred: 1) she hired a white "maid" to care
for her children; 2) she initiated and eventually dropped a $200,000
suit against a neighbor woman who called her "a tramp" in the hearing
of her children when they were confronting one another about noise
that the Morrison children were making; 3) she began to write.

Sula (1974) shifted her concerns from childhood to a more
complex view of life. In the second book she used the viewpoints of
two women alternately. By 1979, the time of this interview, she had
reduced her time in the office to one day a week and was keeping her
evenings carefully protected so that she could write as much as
possible. All the while she operated on a "Don't ask; do" principle.

Without asking Knopf publishers, she took a job at Yale teaching a fiction writing class on Fridays. When her immediate superior at Knopf once called a meeting on Friday, she then announced she would be unable to attend because she was teaching on Fridays at Yale.

She lived in Queens for five years, and in 1970 bought a house outside Manhattan, in Rockland County. In 1979 she switched her children to public schools in Spring Valley. Before that, they had gone first to the United Nations International School and then to Walden School.

She knew only her maternal grandparents when she was growing up. They had been sharecroppers from Alabama. Her father's parents, who lived in Georgia, had already died. Her great grandmother was an Indian who was given 88 acres of land by the government during Reconstruction (p. 54). Somehow her land got legally entangled as a result of debts which her son (TM's grandfather) owed but didn't know he owed. Ultimately he lost the land he had inherited and wound up working for those to whom he lost out.

Asked if she would consider marrying again, TM admits to liking "the minutiae" of being married, but not having "to go where they say" (p.56). Diane Johnson, reviewing the books of TM and Gayl Jones, finds that the characters in the latter's work are twisted and even grotesque: "...they entirely concern black people who violate, victimize, and kill each other. . . . No relationships endure, and all are founded on exploitation" (p. 56). In an effort to make a summary judgement about the books she was reviewing, Johnson concludes they are lacking in very substantial ways. The novels do not have "the complicating features of meaning or moral commitment" (p. 56) that she believes are essential to great literature. The reason for the large audience for TM's work is that readers consistently avoid analyzing the brutal or the bizarre in her fiction. Johnson raises the psychologically complicated possibility that TM's "largely white audience thrills voyeuristically to the black magic she invokes" and that by so doing, she is in an unintentional but insidious way confirming white fears about blacks by both shocking and fascinating them (p. 58).

To conclude this interview, TM insists that her concern is for "the elaborately socialized world of black people" (p.58), a world she left behind when she grew up and moved and which may regrettably no longer exist anywhere as a result of the way modern life is lived constantly in transition.

"Person To Person." *Black Seeds* (London, England) 1 (1979): 28-29.

25. Weatherby, W.J. "'As Far Back as I'm Interested.'" *GW* 119 (August 27, 1978): 21.

Without doubt, TM's own career has benefitted from the patterns of American corporate merger which made Random House one of the three leading publishers in the country. Physically TM now is ensconced atop the RCA skyscraper and works as a senior editor for the house which distributes her fiction when it is put into print by Knopf. Yet even as she has climbed to the rarified atmosphere occupied by other high-level executives, TM manages to write a kind of fiction which is uniquely accessible to large numbers of readers and which makes her both popular and artistically successful.

She has distanced herself from the writing fashions of the '60's, and by trimming her prose of the "rhetoric and haranguing" of those days has been able to contact her particular audience: black, rural people. She is not interested in the "fashionable search for ancestral roots" (p.21), but maintains a nurturing contact with members of her own family back to her great-great-grandmother: "that's as far back as I'm interested" (p. 21).

As a businesswoman who also loves good books, TM respects small publishers (not the Random Houses of the profession) for producing "elegant" books despite serious distribution problems. She says she has no trouble at all keeping the political maneuvering and the editorial objectivity of her business position separate from the passionate involvement required by her own fiction writing.

1981

26. LeClair, Thomas. "The Language Must Not Sweat: A Conversation With Toni Morrison." *NRep* 184 (March 21, 1981): 25-29.

English professor LeClair seeks TM out at her Random House office just after the publication of *TB* and suggests the most unique feature of her work is her special fictional voice, what she calls her "address," a voice so shaped by literal love of word making that it gives her an almost physical relationship to language.

On the meaning of the writing process for her, TM claims it is a way to shape and order experience, a way to work for herself and by herself, and an artist's medium which--like movement for a dancer-- gives her a sense of gravity and space and time (p. 25).

Her function, she sees as creating what she calls "peasant literature," or "village literature" for the tribe who are her people (p. 26) and whose old ways are being obliterated by the modern urban disconnectedness of the cities to which they are moving. So, like the novelist of the middle class in the 19th century, who served a needful social function by defining the class for itself, TM now serves a similar function for a people who "are being devoured" (p. 26), and who in the process risk losing all sense of who they have been as well as the rich language which has been theirs. Loss of a sense of community undercuts the old myths too, such as the myth of flying which she makes central to *SOS,* and the African myth of the tar lady which she uses as the focus of *TB.* The tar baby carries multiple meanings: it is a device used by the white man to catch a rabbit; it is a name used by whites for black girls; and it is an allusion to the tar pit as a holy place, to the material used for building, and to the way a black woman can hold things together. That kind of mix of history and prophecy TM feels compelled to "dust off" and renew in the minds of tenuously connected modern villagers.

Asked what is distinctive about her own fiction, TM answers that it is the language, which must appear effortless and yet reveal the playful experimentational quality of black speech. She feels she serves a conservative function by keeping alive the knowledge of five different present tenses, of African etymologies ("hip," "the dozens"), and of adverbless dialogue (p. 27).

Because her audience is the tribe, her literature "peasant literature" with its language based in unique cultural assumptions, TM's artistic function may have levels of appreciation unavailable to any but the initiated. Her writing is for " the people," which in her view means only black people. If the writing has a "universal" quality, that is because it was first successful on a specific, particular level.

Those who praise TM's gift for humor and satire may be surprised to learn that, in her own estimation, she works more nearly in the tragic mode (about melancholy relationships, catharsis, revelations) than in the comic. That she writes in the elevated mode of tragedy accounts in part for the "extraordinary" quality of her characters. So too does her love of and respect for the past, when people were more interesting than now, when they exhibited more excesses, when they conformed less--like a Sula. And the community permitted the nonconformity. It discourages her that today's community of readers, lacking awareness, says, "Who are these people?" with whom the author is so passionate and engaged.

"Naming" in *SOS* was a means for TM to acknowledge traditions also. Characters have names that are not their own (evidence of the cultural orphanage), they have biblical names (evidence of the black awe for scripture and their ability to distort it for their own ends), and pre-Christian names (evidence of a mix of cosmologies). Milkman Dead's learning the significance of his name gives him power (p. 28).

Visual qualities are very crucial to TM. She often works outward from a metaphorical conception to the structure of a scene, and on occasion she conceives of whole novels as metaphors. *Sula* she thinks of "as a cracked mirror, fragments and pieces we have to see independently and put together" (p. 28). *TBE* is represented metaphorically by the notion of a grade school primer story, its simple, happy family a civilized frame for the chaos of black life narrated therein (p. 29).

The theme of the mask is important in black literature in general and essential to *TB* because white people do not see others for what they are, and so "you never tell a white person the truth" (p. 29).

Finally, TM notes her dissatisfaction with contemporary criticism, which she believes is "following post-modern fiction into self-consciousness, talking about itself as though it were the work of art" (p. 29). She yearns for a critic who "understands /her/ work or is prepared to understand it" (p.29), because better criticism can help produce better fiction.

27.   Wilson, Judith. "A Conversation With Toni Morrison." *Ess* (July, 1981): 84-86, 128ff.

After the success of *TBE, Sula,* and *SOS,* and having made the cover of *Newsweek* with the publication of *TB*, TM's militancy is now evident as never before. Yet she insists black women must reconcile their need for professional self-expression with the equally valuable need to foster "the nurturing thing," (p. 86) and to remain in touch with, taking care of, the ancestors. A whole village has to raise a child, not one or even two parents. Having a profession is an admirable aim, yet it must be made to dovetail with the demands on women to nurture families.

TB, although critics see it as a radical departure for TM, is in fact "a very classic, peasant story" using nature as a chorus and employing the "call-and-response" technique of performer and audience.

Black women writers tend to be addressing other black women. This gives their work a unique style different from that of white women writers (confessional) and black male writers (confrontational).

As an editor, TM feels unfulfilled because the works of authors to whom she has been committed (Toni Cade Bambara, Gayl Jones) did not sell in numbers comarable to her own. This is not an indication of the quality of their writing, but rather reflects the reluctance of the market place to accept black writing. Once a "relentlessly Black" book realizes huge commercial success, others will surely follow. Therein lies the political importance of TM's insisting she is not a "plain old writer" but a black writer (p. 130).

TB is a political novel in that Jadine, the tar baby, was created by white, western culture. In TM's judgement, it is not as political, however, as *SOS*. Although she is aware of readers wanting concrete, unambiguous resolutions, TM could not provide that in *TB*, where the central conflict is cultural, not sexual. It could not be resolved by having the man and woman go away happily together in the end.

What black women have to retain is their generations-long capacity to handle the problems of work and family. Doing both, doing what one has to without complaining--that is being grown up.

Her technical aim is to write in "a" black style, so that her work becomes as distinctive to a literary sensibility as the music of a black musician is to someone knowledgeable about that art. A black style has an aural quality, its narrative spine is "biblical and meandering" (p. 134). Black culture, whether in the American South or West or in New York City, is basically the same.

Whatever her next book turns out to be, it will be different from the others and simultaneously about the same thing: being black in this country.

1983

28. Bonetti, Kay. "Toni Morrison Interview." *American Audio Prose Library*, Columbia, MO, May, 1983, 78 minutes.

The mix of racial and social attitudes which could be found in northern and southern Ohio had an abiding influence on Toni Morrison's beliefs--as did her own mother and father. The latter was a "racist" of the sort who assumed his own race to be morally superior and considered whites constitutionally incapable of "transcending the qualities of their own species." TM was shocked by that when young and more inclined to her mother's optimistic view, presuming that human relations could be improved through education, but now, later in her life, she shares her father's less hopeful attitude and has come to accept the truth of how entrenched and institutionalized racist ideas are in this society.

Her own interest in writing began late, when she was over 30. She would like to put labels such as "women's writing" out of business, in order to allow people to luxuriate in what is original in that writing without denying all that has gone before. Yet she definitely considers herself a "black writer." TM intends to reproduce the artlessness, the effortlessness, the non-bookness of black people. Structurally she works for a circularity and openness. As regards voice, she wants a quality of oral address that retains the originality of black speech and invites the reader to participate in the creative process (as the audience does through the "call and response" in a church service).

Her novels begin with the "germ" of an idea (black people being able to fly; the tar baby) and develop through a process of rigorous self-discovery. Mel Brooks' film company has bought the rights to *TB* and Toni Cade Bambara is doing the screenplay.

TM herself did the book and lyrics for a musical comedy called *New Orleans*, concerning the closing of Storyville by the Navy in 1917. Though that part of New Orleans and the more staid, Christian

34

black community were at odds, the two sides were sealed by the jazz music that was released into the culture at the time, traversed the whole country, and became one of the bases on which modernism developed.

That fiction must remain apolitical in order to be true art is in itself an insidious, political assertion which Morrison denies. Latin American literature, the strongest national literature now being written, stands as an impressive example of writing that is highly political and high art.

29.   McKay, Nellie. "An Interview With Toni Morrison." *ConL* 24, no.4 (1983): 413-29.

Here TM acknowledges her kinship to black women of earlier eras, the "culture bearers" for the group. In her own family, responsibility for narrative arts was shared jointly and without conflict by both genders, thus she got an admirable model of self-assurance from her mother, who never felt the need to hide her talents from white society.

Using hindsight, she says it may be possible to describe an evolutionary trend in her work. Certainly "the writing gets better" (p. 417) as she gains confidence through problem solving. Her physical canvasses have gotten larger as she moves to include men in increasingly significant ways because their lives are led with an "outward, adventuresome" rhythm. In *TB* she intended to force characters to examine truly what they are, and to facilitate that, she cut them off from traditional support systems or escape routes.

When beginning a book, she tries to create a trying circumstance, and she claims she generally knows the ending of her books, but not the middle.

As novelist, she bristles at the suggestion that in her fiction she should serve political purposes by creating brave, wonderful women and "stable" black men.   "/That/ would bore me to death" (419) she admits, and notes that any number of her male figures (Milkman, Ajax, Macon Dead, Sidney) reveal a genuine mix of good and bad that makes them more intriguing than if they had been handled with clear resolutions.   What interests TM are character features such as complexity, the ability to survive (even when possessed of agonizing self-knowledge), and the effect of duress on characters. Pilate, for instance, has strengths neither her daughter Hannah nor her granddaughter Eva possess, because Pilate experienced a good, nurturing relationship with a man and was better for it.

Besides subtlety in characterization, TM aims to produce with her writing the strong visceral, emotional response in an audience that is typically generated by oral literature of old. She wants the reader to think about basic conflict issues such as being black and having a sense of authentic personhood. Such issues are raised by the culture more nearly than by the fact of gender. So in *TB* the problems Jadine and Son face are not so much gender-based as culture-based. What becomes important is that the characters "press toward knowledge" even if that knowledge comes "at the expense of happiness" (p. 424). So the book ends with Jadine understanding better why she is running. Structurally the close of the work complements its opening in that it presents readers with a kind of metaphorical birth for Son, combining the sound of the old folk tale ("lickety split") with the evolutionary sight of a man crawling, walking, running, always with growing confidence.

Committed as she is to the primacy of cultural issues, TM yearns for critics who can read her works in terms of the basic structure out of which they grow: black cosmology. Criticism which sees her as "like" Faulkner or Joyce mistake her major intention. She is trying to express in literature what survives in isolation in the black community/tribe and "has probably only been fully expressed in music" (p. 426). To capture in literature the story black people have to tell requires an oral quality and a meandering, open ended sort of folk structure that comes from a material which is constantly being reimagined and reorganized by its countless retellers. Hence her writings combine the earthy sense of the practical and shrewd real world folks with abiding respect for the supernatural--the latter being often considered "discredited knowledge" these days. Milkman Dead's odyssey illustrates how the two kinds of knowledge must be combined. Milkman acquires a hard-nosed kind of knowledge from Guitar and other male figures in *SOS,* and an ennobling kind of mystical wisdom from Pilate and the other women figures. Together the two sets of information give him a sense of harmony as a human being.

30.   Tate, Claudia. "Toni Morrison." *Black Women Writers At Work.* Edited by Claudia Tate. New York: Continuum, 1983, pp. 117-31.

Being black and female was very much a determining concept in *Sula* because friendship between women simply had not been dealt with. The midwest is where TM's "beginnings" are, but she considers black culture to be very much the same no matter where it is found.

TM discusses her writing habits, how she makes time for her work, how she deals with writer's block, and the mysterious value of using cliches. She indicates her frustration with insensitive critics both white and black, and asserts that just as she feels qualified to discuss authors such as Emily Dickinson, so too should any honest scholar of another race be capable of analyzing the preoccupations of black writers. Universal human concerns underlie such work.

At other points in the interview, though, TM discusses in some detail not the universal qualities of blacks, but the particular ones: a lack of fear of death or of being different; an awareness of difference before similarity; a predisposition not to see things and people stereotypically. Furthermore, she reveals her conviction that there are substantial gender differences in writing, not especially that women write differently from men, but that black women write differently from white women. Black men and white men, she says, write very much alike. Regarding male vs. female writing, TM notes that men "want to change things and women probably don't" (p.123).

She comments on the rhythmic, circular structure of *TBE* and *Sula,* as contrasted with the linear, outward progression of *SOS,* noting as she does her aim to force readers to be "participatory" with the literary experience and to provide emotions and coloring themselves.

The type of character which particularly interests her is the misunderstood, fearless, somewhat "wild" figure who resists controls. Cholly, Ajax, Guitar, and Sula are examples. Various "levels" of the pariah figure in her work are discussed as the author talks about social responses to evil.

TM's writing process involves laborious revison to achieve an oral quality and to eliminate editorializing. She intends to show, to make the reader see, and no more.

Finally, TM discusses critical responses to her work, how those often surprise and sometimes disappoint her with what she considers inaccurate readings. She is not interested, she says, in reworking her fiction for the cinema. Material success achieved through her writing has not changed the essentials of her life.

1984

31.   "Rootedness: The Ancestor as Foundation." *Black Women Writers, 1950-1980.*   Edited by Mari Evans.   New York: Anchor Press/Doubleday, 1984: 339-45.
    The piece is a combined interview-essay. Mari Evans set out to collect written responses to a series of questions put to each author included in the collection. TM agreed to respond only if the interview were done by either Nikki Giovanni or Eleanor Traylor. The latter conducted the interview, then, but her questions have been omitted. Though it has a decidedly fragmentary quality, the essay contains important information about her view of the function of fiction and the role of the writer.
    TM begins by commenting on the problem a writer faces by having to be both a "representative of the tribe and in it" (p. 339). She looks somewhat nostalgically at a time when "an artist could have a tribal or racial sensibility and an individual expression of it" (p. 339), and says that the black church service retains a remnant of that. There individuals can respond as individuals, yet they keep the security of the group, the "community." Lacking that context as a writer, she

works extremely hard to keep her own life as private as possible so that her work can be done seriously.

With characteristic insight, TM asserts here that blacks need the novel now more than ever. She bases this belief on her understanding that fiction "is for the class that wrote it" (p. 340), which originally meant the middle class. The purpose of such fiction, in the 18th century and for a long while thereafter, was to give readers all the rules they needed for social behavior. Contemporary black audiences do not need the novel for manners, but to provide a new generation with "those classical, mythological archetypal stories that we heard years ago" (p. 340) but which young people are not hearing any longer. Extended families are clearly the exception now; children grow up and when they do, they leave; families disperse in search of work or more hospitable living. Through her fiction, TM intends to present problems, not their answers. She wants audiences to be "moved," sometimes literally to stand and shout or cry in response to her fiction, sometimes less literally, to be changed or modified by their experience with it. Absolutely essential to her purpose, she insists, is "the affective and participatory relationship between the artist or the speaker and the audience" (p. 341).

One of the techniques she uses to create that participatory response is a choral quality. In each of her four novels the strategy is used: in *TBE* it is the "I" narrator; in *Sula* it is the town as character; in *SOS* it is the community in both parts of the novel; and in *TB* it is nature itself.

She explicitly denies the usefulness of a uniquely feminist critical stance. As regards her own work, she wants critics to condemn or to praise her writing on the basis of criteria that are relevant to the culture out of which she writes. She says she does not appreciate being evaluated by a critical system which applies evaluative standards derived "from other paradigms" (p. 342).

More explicitly here than on any previous occasion, TM articulates what she means by "black literature." She defines negatively first, and shows that in her view such literature is not necessarily writing by or about black people. It is instead writing that evidences certain unique qualities, among them the following:

1) an acceptance of the supernatural and also a rootedness in the real world;

2) a special sort of cosmology that allows one to look at the world in pragmatic terms but also to accept the relevance of "superstition and magic, which is another way of knowing things" (p. 342);

3) a willingness to use that which the dominant culture calls "discredited knowledge," discredited because those who know it are;

4) a unique oral quality;

5) a literature that attempts to evoke a participatory relationship between reader and work;

6) a reliance on a particular kind of character that might be called "an ancestor:" those "timeless people whose relationships to the characters are benevolent, instructive, and protective and /who/ provide a certain kind of wisdom"(p. 343);

7) an especially communal way of looking at the artist. This communal view of the speaker of oral art grows out of a people's sense of whether "the writer is one of them" (p.343), and not separated, isolated. The writer of black literature is identified with "an implied 'we' in the narration" (p. 343).

Again responding to a question about feminist implications in her work, TM denies that Pilate's gender is the most important thing about her. What really counts is that Pilate is this ancient wisdom which can be found in "the ancestor" and without which a family, a community, or a people are lost. Thus she does not want to define as superior any model of critical inquiry that is either feminist and overlooks the importance of the males, or masculine and ignores the crucial function of females in literature.

Her work is "political" insofar as she intends it to be "about the village or the community or about you" (p. 344). She does not aim at any sort of solipsistic or ingrown focus on self. But while the literature is political and relevant as noted above, it must never degenerate into mere harangue; it must be beautiful; aesthetic considerations are all.

PART IV
ESSAYS, ARTICLES, AND BOOKS ON GENERAL TOPICS

32.   Bischoff, Joan. "The Novels of Toni Morrison: Studies in Thwarted
        Sensitivity." *SBL* 6, #3 (1975): 21-23.

        In each of her first two novels, TM takes up the Jamesian notion
of a precocious female protagonist suffering from the lack of a healthy
outlet for her aspiration. Pecola Breedlove escapes into madness, Sula
(a reworking of the same material) into amoral self-reliance.

        Pecola is uniquely vulnerable to psychic harm because she is
considered ugly, is relatively friendless, and has no sense of self-
worth. Her budding sensitivity a source of pain, Pecola tries to make
herself disappear, eventually retreating into overwhelming madness.
Sula Peace is slightly blemished physically by a birthmark but has
evolved an interior void that makes her much less becoming. The
townspeople consider her evil, yet by the novel's close her friend Nel
weeps inconsolably over her loss. Sula is an example of potential
humanity stifled by lack of fostering (p. 22). She seeks satisfaction
in casual affairs, impulsive actions, childhood mischief--all without
attachments, and as a consequence she dies completely alone. The fact
that she embraces her loneliness ("my lonely is mine..." p. 22) is
small affirmation. She cannot be hurt, but neither has she any
pleasure.

33.   Blake, Susan L. "Toni Morrison." *DLB, Afro-American Fiction
        Writers After 1955*. Edited by Thadious M. Davis and Trudier Harris.
        Detroit, Michigan: Gale Research Company, 1984. Vol. 33, pp. 187-
        199.

        Popular and critically acclaimed, feminist and spokesperson for
black people generally, TM is the most notable anomaly among
contemporary black writers.

        Chloe Anthony Wofford, second of four children, grew up in a
household that believed "black people were the humans of the globe"
and doubted "the quality and existence of white humanity" (p. 188).
Her formal education acquainted her with the classics of western
literature, her informal learning (social life at Howard University,
traveling the American South with a group of university actors)
focused her cultural identity as a black woman.

        Generally her novels use a dialectical approach, playing
opposing arrays of values against one another. Various ways of being
black or female are illustrated throughout her novels, and a failed
quest for cultural identity in one work (*TBE*) is set against a
triumphant search in another (*SOS*).

        TBE is a novel of failed initiation. Pecola Breedlove does not
successfully negotiate the rites of passage into maturity; she becomes a
victim instead of a viable member of society, and her story "is also the
story of her family and her culture" (p. 189), in that many of the other
characters in the book have been victimized in their turn. Pecola's

madness is a foregone conclusion because she cannot believe she can be lovely, lovable, or happy without becoming what she is not, "someone white" (p. 189).

The Morrison dialectic is evident in the structure of *TBE* , where positive and negative versions of the theme are set in opposition through TM's parodying fairy tale concepts of life with the demoralizing realities of Pecola's existence. If the image of the "ideal" white family is brutally misleading and that of the Breedloves is mean and destructive, the example of the MacTeers (who resemble the Woffords) provides a workable synthesis. Claudia and Frieda are nurtured and protected by their parents and as a result develop self-images which are proud but not vain, assertive but not intrusive. The MacTeer girls lose their innocence in part through Pecola, and their acquired wisdom is undercut by their awareness of complicity in her unhappy fate.

The author's view of moral ambiguity is extended in *Sula*. Sacrificial and/or harmful events blur and thus disturb a reader's inclination to type characters as good or evil. Focused on the relation between Nel Wright and Sula Peace, the novel examines various examples of good and bad behavior as it chronicles two stories of female self-discovery. Nel is conventionally good; she endorses the Bottom's standards of behavior. Sula repudiates everything about Medallion and conventionally defined values. She is, like death, the "unknown and uncontrollable in...life" (pp. 191-192), and even her last line of dialogue, spoken after her death, attests to her being "the representative of another world" (p. 192).

Critical reception to *Sula* as a truthful representation of black life done in surreal terms was generally favorable. Addison Gayle, Jerry Bryant, and Sarah Blackburn faulted the work, though, for its use of stereotypes, its tone of detachment, and its lacking "immediacy."

The relevance of black history is an abiding concern for TM. In 1974, two months after the appearance of *Sula*, Random House brought out *The Black Book*, "which, though her name appears nowhere on it, was Toni Morrison's idea and very much her project" (p. 192). She conceived the book as a way to acknowledge the countless persons whose contributions comprise the whole weave of black history, and, perhaps more significantly, to rescue this kind of folk history from the "faddism" of mass culture and narrowly conceived political movements.

In *SOS,* as in *The Black Book*, TM works to rediscover old myths. Milkman must accomplish his unique rite of passage, must earn his identity, by discovering his connection with his ancestors ("Solomon," "Sing," "the lost farm," are all from TM family history). That is accomplished both through Milkman's undergoing a literal journey from Michigan southward into country occupied by his forebears, and by the process of his "imaginative journey out of self" (p. 193) which transforms and matures him.

Again TM employs a dialectical approach, setting the role of Milkman's materialistic father against that of his humanistic Aunt Pilate. Milkman and his best friend, Guitar, are also a contrasted pair whose attitudes toward themselves as individuals and toward race serve as models of evolving consciousness.

The fairy tale quest and Afro-American folklore form the structural basis of the book. Milkman's obligation is like that of the fairy tale character who earns the assistance of magical guides by learning to share a bread crust or to love a crone. TM also owes an explicit debt to the Georgia Writers' Project collection *Drums and Shadows* for the story of legendary flying Africans.

As might be expected about a work that attracts tremendous attention, *SOS* sparked divided response from critics. Some considered it an inaccurate representation of black life, and a book that was by any measure less original, less successful than earlier work. Others viewed *SOS* as more ambitious, and certainly it was a huge financial success.

In *TB* Morrison's most overtly political sentiments are evident. The book is "an allegory of colonialism" (p. 194) in which the "characters represent various stages in the relationship between colonizer and colonized" (p. 195). White figures and black, ranging from the imperialistic employer to workers on the estate, to "in house" servants, to near-members of the white power structure all exhibit degrees of dependence. Eventually Valerian's empire crumbles and is taken over by the servants, just as the buildings will be by the West Indian jungle.

The conflict between Jadine and the "primitive" William Green, emblematically named "Son," is carried on in racial and gender and cultural terms. In their on-again-off-again relationship are dramatized different ways of being black or a woman (or man) or culturally authentic. The author respects Son for his integrity and his maleness; she is unsympathetic to Jadine for her being a failed black woman.

Critical responses to *TB* were divided. The best ones called the book "intricate," "moving," and "ambitious." The worst flogged it for being polemical, its content confusing, its style obscure.

TB is a kind of recapitulation of TM's earlier work. Individual identity vs. black identity, material vs. familial values, relatedness vs. independence all marked the first three books and also become the substance of the fourth. In every one a recurring irony is clear: true freedom lies in commitment to others; what passes for independence is actually the trap of solitariness.

But as the scope of TM's fiction enlarges, its focus narrows. In *TBE,* the young girls had to define themselves in relation to white society; in *TB* the grown women's many conflicts are all "subsumed in the very personal conflict between self and sexuality" (p. 196). The last work is morally simpler, and the statement it makes is imposed from without. Nor are symbolism and content successfully fused as in *TBE* and *SOS.* Thus although the three earlier works are totally credible as imaginative fiction, *TB* is not. *TBE* is a coherent antifairy tale, *SOS* a rediscovered legend. But *TB* is merely "an analogy" (p. 197).

At her best, TM writes a kind of fabulist prose that successfully negotiates the task of walking the line between authorial intrusion and moralizing. In *TB* she does not maintain the balance between the fabulous and the specific, and so the novel becomes a rather simple fable.

In part, the tendency toward fable in TM's fiction is a result of her conscious attempt to produce "village literature" that clarifies for her readers how they should relate to one another and "survive whole" (p. 197) through love.

Hers is a type of fiction which, "like quiltmaking, is a folk art . . . both pieced and highly patterned" (p. 198). In that sense she is simultaneously the most contemporary and the most old-fashioned of black writers.

34. Christian, Barbara. "Community and Nature: The Novels of Toni Morrison." *JEthS* 7, no. 4 (Winter, 1980): 65-78.

TM's *TBE, Sula,* and *SOS* all bear upon black communities which affirm a unique concept of Nature (p.65). Individual characters such as Pecola Breedlove or Sula or Milkman Dead are the products of the communal relations which surround them, their values established by those communities. Consequently "place is as important as the human actors" (p.65), and changes in setting drastically alter values which give characters' lives coherence. The southern communities from which they came supported those characters better than the sterile urban contexts into which they migrated.

Pauline Breedlove's poisonous sense of self attests to the lack of tradition--usually associated with the land--which results when a community is separated from Nature. In *TBE* the natural order is inverted, because natural concepts of beauty and of family are terribly disordered. *Sula* opens with the sardonically humorous myth of the Bottom's beginnings created in order to teach the black community a functional realpolitik: "the only way one can defeat evil is by outlasting it" (p. 67). This philosophy gets transferred to Sula too, a character whose evil the people attempt to overcome by outlasting her. Natural concepts of woman are inappropriate for Sula, so the Bottom assigns her the role of witch. Then by uniting against her, they affirm their own ironic sense of community. In the end, many of the folks in that town are physically destroyed by the forces of nature for insisting on mere survival (p. 71). The downside of a philosophy which is nature based is that it can create such a strong sense of insularity related to place that traditions become dangerously static, thus likely to turn obsolete (p. 67).In *SOS* rural, land based values of Milkman's grandfather are contrasted with the materialistic ones of his urban father. Macon wants to subvert the original generative notions of nature by owning it. This has the effect of transforming nature into a thing. His example is offset by that of Pilate, his sister, who retains an appreciation for the land she came from (p.72). Frequently TM uses natural concepts to structure her materials (p.73). She stresses time (seasons, cycles of growth and decay, chronology) and the inversions of natural order caused by human society. Significant action is related to primal metaphors involving fire (Eva and Hannah), water (Sula), earth (Nel's solidity; the need to bury the bones of grandfather Macon Dead), and air (Ajax's dream of flight; Milkman's achievement of the dream).

35. Christian, Barbara. "The Concept of Class in the Novels of Toni Morrison." *Black Feminist Criticism.* New York, Oxford, Toronto, Sydney, Paris, Frankfurt: Athene Series, Pergamon Press, 1985, pp. 71-80.

Works of fiction by black women from Frances Harper to TM have been studied by critics as expressions of the condition of being black and female. Another aspect of the definition of "woman" grows out of an individual's being measured by the standards of "class."

The standard by which particular characters are assessed is the 18th century image of the ideal southern lady: beautiful, white, nonworking, upper middle class, a mother, and supportive of her husband. Whether such an ideal in fact ever existed is immaterial. Ms. Christian presumes the image "was, and probably still is, seen as the standard toward which a woman should aspire" (p. 72). Such a standard excludes black women categorically, since racism makes of them a lower class, and white aesthetic standards make them ugly. Although biologically female, they are precluded from achieving the standard of womanhood.

Novels by black women have consistently challenged this concept of class as a definition of womanhood. Francis Harper (*Iola Leroy*), Zora Neale Hurston (*Their Eyes Were Watching God*), and Ann Petry (*The Street*) call the class aspects of womanhood seriously into question.

All of TM's novels consider the definition in terms of race and class assumptions. *TBE* presents the reader an entire spectrum of female characters ranging from poor and ugly Pecola on the bottom to the "girl-doll" daughter of the white family for which Pecola's mother works at the top. Between these extremes are arranged Maureen Peal (light-skinned princess), Geraldine (darker, aristocratic socially, with a frigid, middle class sexual morality), and the MacTeer girls' mother (poor-but-loving). The whole book is about class distinctions and the need for a sense of superiority which threatens self-worth.

In *Sula* Helen /Helene/ Wright is the image of the lady: full of hypocrisy. Even Nel's sense of womanhood is based in part on her supporting a "failed" man. And Sula fiercely resists any and all definitions of womanhood that her community recognizes--especially the trait which says the ideal woman nurtures the community by bearing children and supports her man "sexually, emotionally, or financially" (p. 76).

SOS is not focused primarily on the relation of gender and class so much as on male self-knowledge. Yet within the novel's larger concerns looms the image of Ruth Foster Dead as a "grotesque" version of the ideal southern lady image. And Pilate is a female nurturer, it is true, but one who is "totally beyond class distinctions" (p. 78).

TB is TM's most contemporary novel and her most dramatic presentation of male-female relations. Jadine Childs exemplifies female independence, and, not surprisingly, her values are almost exactly those "of the white male world" (p. 78). Jadine denies the worth of female nurturing and of meaningful relations within a community. In her, class has become "more critical than racial bonds" (p.79), and woman is seen to be adopting patriarchal values. Her lover, Son, is a man of no class who opts ultimately for mythic (not economic) virtues. Unfortunately both those characters appear to represent dead ends.

Certainly TM's whole body of work asks basic, urgent questions about the interrelatedness of race, sex, and class (p. 79).

* *Black Women Novelists: The Development of a Tradition, 1892-1976.* Cited below as item 61.

36. Clark, Norris B., III. "The Black Aesthetic Reviewed: A Critical Examination of the Writings of Imamu Amiri Baraka, Gwendolyn Brooks, and Toni Morrison." Ph.D. diss., Cornell University, 1980. *DAI.* 41 (1980): 1053A.

Social history in the 1970's produced a self-conscious aesthetic movement organized around the concept of "a rebirth into blackness." This study considers the politically and socially generated work of Imamu Amiri Baraka and Gwendolyn Brooks to be aesthetic failures even if tested by criteria of the Black Aesthetic. TM's fiction, on the contrary, is aesthetically valid, primarily because it unites the black American experience with mankind's universal experience. In sum, the Black Aesthetic does not exist, and that ideology has failed to effect either its literary or political objectives.

37. Davis, Cynthia. "Self, Society, and Myth in Toni Morrison's Fiction." *ConL* 23 (1982): 323-42.

Thematically central to TM's first three novels is the search for a myth adequate to articulate the reality of experience. Her fictional black world is surrounded by and yet invisible to white society in a way that is highlighted by insidious patterns of misnaming. Black reality is not eliminated by the misnaming of characters and streets and neighborhoods, but it is distorted so that it loses its independent reality.

Sarte's discussion of how "the Look" shapes human relations provides Ms. Davis with the premises of her approach. Principal characters in *TBE* and *Sula* and *SOS* all abdicate their own responsibility to define themselves, by substituting for a sense of self the way they are seen by others (p. 325). More pernicious is the way characters internalize "the Look" of majority culture and then try futilely to live up to it.

For TM, both adopting rigid roles and withdrawing from life altogether are failures, but failures tempered by her recognition of the unnatural position of blacks in a racist society. That society steals black reality and substitutes for it "dead, external classifications for free self-definition" (p.328), until finally there is "a Look with no one behind it" and the models one sees--pin up girls, movie stars--say only that life is being and appearance, but not choice.

Black women face a double dilemma: that of a woman in a patriarchal society, and that of a black in a racist one (p. 329). They become natural scapegoats, from being seen as outsiders and failures, and the objects of violent, frustrated anger in black males as well as occasionally in other black women too. The epitome of the victim is Pecola Breedlove, irredeemably excluded from social reality and going mad fantasizing that her eyes are turning blue and making her acceptable to the world she occupies. Characters who are stronger, like Cholly Breedlove or Sula, may choose the freedom of isolation, but TM's fiction presents that choice as another kind of deprivation. Theirs becomes a kind of outrageous, detached, even cruel freedom that illustrates not a "choosing self, but a lack of self" (p. 333). "Freedom defined as total transcendence lacks the intention and significance that can come from commitment" (p. 333).The ideal quest for self is realized in Milkman Dead, who is depicted in clear mythic terms. He has a miraculous birth, undergoes a quest-journey, and integrates his own ends with his culture's (p. 333). Evidence of his combining the notions of free individual and member of the social group is the novel's ending in which Milkman "flies" toward his dark brother, Guitar, instead of away by himself.

TM discovers mythic possibilities for her characters by allowing them to make significant choices despite a dominating culture which would deny that. And she employs the subtle variations of myth by narrating it so that its problematical complexity remains central. In Milkman's version of the Icarus myth, then, the enlightened black hero confronts divided loyalties: choosing absolute freedom and "flying" away would mean simultaneously denying his social responsibility. TM stubbornly retains the dual stress on true, psychic meaning in her tale, and also on the impact of "necessity" imported by the social order (p. 336).

She is always concerned with the sources of myth and with distinguishing false myths that distort from true myths that illuminate reality, and her use of shifting points of view and multiple perspectives keep the audience from reading her use of myth reductively.

It must be said, though, that her hero tale in *SOS* requires a protagonist who is male, and she readily complies. The females in the novel exist for Milkman (and for the plot) as functions (p. 338), because the myth of heroism in the male line allows women to benefit but not to originate. Even Pilate, female guiding figure and possessed of great intuitive qualities though she is, does not fit the hero mold. She lacks the recognition of meaning which Milkman achieves, and so the novel underlines the difficulty of the heroic mode for a woman. Milkman, on the contrary, discovers his own identity even as he finds a connection to society. He rejects his father in a classic act of rebellion, but he embraces his forefathers. That is impossible for women like Pilate, who have not recovered their heroic female line so as to be capable of serving an integrative heroic function . Women still need a new myth--which Morrison has not yet set down.

38. Gaston, Karen C. "The Theme of Female Self-Discovery in the Novels of Judith Rossner, Gail Godwin, Alice Walker, and Toni Morrison." Ph.D. diss., Auburn University. *DAI.* 41 (1980): 1053A.

This study of four authors looks at the way their writing explores the theme of female self-discovery. Providing resistance to such discovery are cultural pressures such as marriage myths, movies, literature, guilt, irresponsibility, and even personal fear.

Rossner, the most traditional of the four, proposes domestic solutions. Godwin's characters abandon the traditional and rely on their own internal resources. Walker's protagonists return from solitary quests to participate in communal sharing. Morrison is the most ambitious. She works to present black as well as female identity problems. Her novels turn out to be paradoxical, as characters develop self-awareness and also admit the need for a nurturing community. Pilate Dead is her "prototypical female figure" (p. 1053A).

39. Grimes, Johnanna L. "The Function of Oral Tradition in Selected Afro-American Fiction." Ph.D. diss., Northwestern University. *DAI.* 41 (1980): 2604A.

This study examines how folklore (oral tradition, including folk tales, legend, anecdote, folk song, folk belief, and reminiscence) is used in the work of Zora Neale Hurston, Leon Forrest, Albert Murray, and TM. Hurston's *Their Eyes Were Watching God* employs traditional material to shape character, theme and technique. Forrest in his *There is a Tree More Ancient Than Eden* draws on folk traditions to create the essence of his style. Murray's *Train Whistle Guitar* uses orally molded, symbolic characters. Morrison in *TBE, Sula*, and *SOS* uses folk material for characters (Eva, Sula, Ajax) and in the construction of narrative (quest motif in SOS).

40. Harris, Jessica. "Toni Morrison." *Ess* 7 (December, 1976): 54, 56, 90-92.

An interview-article focusing on TM's efforts to balance her three careers as mother, editor, and writer. She refuses to talk about her ex-husband--so as not to pain her two sons, ages 15 and 11--and notes that being a single parent one must be the most complete person possible. Commitment to her children is her first priority.

As Random House editor, TM deals with every step in the publishing process. Henry Dumas is the author she edited whom she considers the most naturally talented, but she also mentions particular skills of Richard Durham (biographer of Muhammed Ali), Angela Davis, Tony Cade Bambara, Lucille Clifton, and Gayl Jones, whose works, *Corregidora* and *Eva's Man*, generated considerable controversy because of their unflattering portraits of men. She does not believe black authors need to be handled by black editors, but those authors do want an editor who is culturally knowledgeable.

Commenting on her use of varied voices, TM says when writing for magazines, she speaks as herself. Writing fiction she works for the involved aloofness that makes it possible for her to see and speak as her characters would. The danger of "losing herself" makes TM extremely wary of the media madness that can and does surround the publication of an author's book. The risk is that one may "become the media's creature" (p. 92), a conclusion TM avoids by being rather solitary, and by cultivating a sense of humor as an antidote to illusion.

* Johnson, Diane. "The Oppressor in The Next Room." *NYRB*. Cited below as item 145.

41. Joyner, Nancy Carol. "Toni Morrison." *DLB, American Novelists Since World War II*. Second Series. Edited by James E. Kibler, Jr. Detroit, Michigan: Gale Research Company, 1980. Vol. 6, pp. 243-247.

With three novels published and a fourth nearly completed, TM has earned a prominent place among contemporary black authors, but critical response to her fiction has been mixed because of its "sometimes bizarre content" (p. 243).

Biographical data shows TM's childhood and youth to have been influenced negatively by the racist biases of grandparents and father. She studied western literature, married a Jamaican architect, had two sons, and was divorced--all before doing any of the creative writing that was to become her first novel, *TBE*. Now a senior editor at Random House, she has taught black literature and fiction writing classes at Bard College and at Yale University.

Each of her novels is original in form and content, but all deal with conflict within the black community rather than with the interracial themes one expects in fiction by black males. Technically she favors small, northern settings, creative naming of characters and places, frequent use of folklore and the Bible, violent incidents, and grotesque characters.

Of her artistic purpose, Ms. Morrison says she intends to provide her audiences with the kind of traditional prose narration that orders for them the chaos of their personal experience.

TBE imposes a very contemporary form upon the age old theme of the social misfit who undertakes a quest for beauty. Pecola Breedlove's pathetic story is narrated both personally by her nine year old friend Claudia, and objectively by a third person omniscient observer. It is organized ironically according to the form of a reading primer for elementary children. Scenes of pain and disorder, such as Pecola's being raped by her despairing father and her consequent mad belief that her eyes have become "the bluest of all" and she beautiful as a result, comprise the bulk of the work.

Sula treats the deep, dependent friendship between two black girls who grow up together, and for years share everything. Together they are responsible for the accidental death of an acquaintance, are separated emotionally by an act of sexual disloyalty on the part of the heavily symbolic Sula, and are reunited briefly just before Sula's death. The structure of the narrative is chronological, spanning 45 years, the plot driven by tight cause-effect relations. Yet the book itself denies easy reduction to its thematic essence. Sula and Nel are complementary figures said to be "representing variously order and disorder; rationality and emotion; conventionality and the lack of it; good and evil" (p. 245).

The third book, *SOS,* is TM's "most elaborate, complex, and mature novel thus far" (p. 246). The author's shift in focus is indicted by the hero's being a man, and by the theme being "a search for...identity and roots" (p.246). Milkman Dead begins by looking for gold and concludes by discovering the mythic secret of his family's history: they had an ancestor named Solomon who could fly. The book has autobiographical elements (TM's grandfather was named John Solomon Willis) but is more nearly a black folktale than a work of history.

Uniquely drawn from the black experience though her novels may be, that fiction ultimately "has universal appeal" (p. 246).

42.   Jua, Mai-Nsangli. "Symbolic Space: Myth and The Pursuit of Order in The Novels of Toni Morrison." Ph.D. diss., SUNY Buffalo, 1984. *DAI.* 46 (1985): 2528-A.

Symbolic spaces (North, South, Mountain, Valley, Island, Sea) contain the key to the question of identity in TM's fiction. Narratives move in circular ways around such spaces and in so doing clarify the sense of self.

43.　Lee, Dorothy H. "The Quest For Self: Triumph and Failure in the Works of Toni Morrison." *Black Women Writers 1950-1980*. Edited by Mari Evans. New York: Anchor Press/Doubleday, 1984, pp.346-360.

TM's novels are unified by a recurring concern with the notion of community and its shaping influence on the individual. The parts of this whole are organized around the quest theme.

TBE is the bleakest of the works and is in Lee's words "a failed quest culminating in madness" (p. 346). Pecola Breedlove is doomed as an individual through no particular fault of her own, but rather because her parents are deeply frustrated in their own lives, utterly lacking in dignity and self-esteem themselves, and thus vengeful toward each other and their children. Pecola's quest for a sense of self is consistently thwarted when she reaches out to peers and to her mother, so she turns of necessity inward, even praying to God to make her disappear. The novel is organized into sections named for the seasons, and in the "Spring" sequence, where readers might expect growth or positive development, Pecola is sexually assaulted by her father, Cholly, in a gesture of "guilt, impotence, and--strangely tenderness" (p. 349). As a result, she is emotionally and psychologically stunted. By the "Summer" sequence she is totally lost in self, a victim of a society that "cleaned itself" on her (p. 349), her pathetic case a "heightened version" of the failure of her parents and other characters in the book (p. 350).

In *Sula* we have another failed figure, this time a woman who wants impossible, contradictory ends: "total personal freedom and /a shared/ relationship with another human being" (p. 350). As novelist, Morrison expands her concerns and covers a 45 year period of time and a whole community structure, but she again uses a scapegoat theme in that Sula is used by the community "as a target for venting their own frustrations" (p. 351). Like the plague of robins that descends on the community as a kind of marker of Sula's return, the latter "is seen by the community as a defilement," thus they "avoid her, exile her, and let her run her course" (p. 352). What Sula apparently seeks so intensely is a wholeness with others; unfortunately she knows no way to realize such except through sexual encounters, and those too are not ultimately satisfying. After the transitory sensation of power experienced in orgasm, Sula knows too keenly the "ending of things" and the "post-coital privateness" that leaves her alone. Ultimately she loses even her best friend, Nel, and also Ajax, whom she had taken as a lover. She herself returns to the community but dies "curiously in boredom."

In *SOS* the main character, Milkman is successful in his quest to know himself and his community. The book works on multiple levels: it is a literal search through different geographical areas; it is a figurative journey "from innocence to awareness" (p. 353); it is a mythic quest which moves "from spiritual death to rebirth...symbolized by his discovery of the power of flight" (p. 353). Milkman's "guides" for his quest are his Aunt Pilate, a model of loving spontaneity, and his friend Guitar, a model of friendship and violent destructiveness. "He proves himself to his family's original village" through a bloodletting combat and a ritual hunting trip (p. 354), and while with his father's and grandfather's peers, he learns the secret of the flying African, Solomon, who "done gone" away home. A children's playground game, ritualistic, melodic, and orally preserved, incorporates historical facts about escaping slaves and allusions to the mythic dream of human flight.

TB plays out "two overlapping, interdependent, and unresolved quests" (p. 355). TM works a number of analogues to the folk tale of the tar baby and the rabbit, but no single reading with one-to-one allegorical equations is satisfactory. Son can be seen as the thieving trickster and Jade the entrapping tar baby. But the ending is an ironic and inverted version of the traditional tale, with Son "like and yet unhappily unlike Brer Rabbit...running lickety-split: down the road but toward the source of his entrapment, alienated from his home, and still 'stuck on' Jade" (p. 356).

The larger concerns of *TB* are indicated by the fact that differences of race and class or caste create the problems facing characters. Jade is presented as "immature" for feeling the need to rate Picasso's masks or Itumba's masks "better" instead of valuable in and of themselves. And her naivete is seen in her "impossible desire to separate her visible identity from a hypothetical, unconnected, interior self" (p. 358). She is said to have "lost her true and ancient properties" and thus to be diminished. She is notably not one of the five women to whom the book is dedicated (p. 358).

In the final analysis, TM indicts all--black and white--for their failure to see individuals as individuals and their inclination to devalue others on the basis of origins and lifestyles. Thus her novelistic concerns can be seen to be focused on "the female especially, ...the Black particularly, and /on/ the human generally" (p. 359).

44. Lee, Valerie G. "The Use of Folklore in Novels By Black Women Writers." *CLAJ* 23 (1979): 266-72.
The dynamics of black culture is represented in fiction by Zora Neale Hurston, TM, and Gayl Jones in a mode of language known as "folktalk." Although generated by women, folktalk focuses on men and on "one of the oldest of universal themes: love and man/women relationships" (p. 266).

The grandmother in Hurston's *Their Eyes Were Watching God* instructs Janie about the strength her being black and a woman will demand of her. The advice is good, but only with her third husband does Janie attain her folk vision of love and men. Janie herself consistently uses folk sayings and metaphors when discussing men with friends. The whole atmosphere of *Their Eyes,* set in an all black community, is essentially established by folktalk related to man-woman relations.

Even in a thoroughly woman's novel like *Sula,* the folktalk among the Peace women concerns menfolk. Despite her saying that black men are "the envy of the world," Sula comes finally to think of her spoiled relationship with Jude in plain, even homely terms borrowed from cooking. Their love, she sees, was "like a pan of syrup kept too long on the stove...leaving only its odor and a hard, sweet sludge..." (p. 270).

Gayl Jones' *Corregidora* is cast neither in romantic terms like Hurston's work nor in earthy ones like Morrison's; it is "bawdy," its folktalk the sexual street language of women preserving the story of their abuse by a Portuguese slave master. Ursa Corregidora, because she cannot reproduce literally, turns to folk music--blues--to express herself on the recurring question: "What's a husband for?" (p. 271).

As independently female as Hurston, Morrison, and Jones are, their literary concerns are with men--as are the concerns of their colleagues Carolyn Rodgers, Stephany, Nikki Giovanni, Gwendolyn Brooks, Sonia Sanchez, and Alice Walker.

45. Malone, Gloria S. "The Nature and Causes of Suffering in the Fiction of Paule Marshall, Kristin Hunter, Toni Morrison, and Alice Walker." Ph.D. diss., Kent State University. *DAI.* 40 (1979): 2063A.

The nature of suffering in the works of these four authors is unique to each; it is also an inescapable fact. Marshall, a Barbadian by heritage, looks at anguish resulting from neo-colonial oppression. In her hands, suffering provides a bond uniting exploited people.

Hunter shows the debilitating effects of urban life, especially that produced by racial intermarriage. In her first three novels, TM exposes the bleakness of life in small towns. Characters are frequently victimized by members of their own families. Walker, the most urgently involved in the plight of black women, demonstrates how each of them bears awesome burdens.

46. Medwick, Cathleen. "Toni Morrison." *Vogue* 171 (April, 1981): 288-289, 330-332.

The interview-essay affords a glimpse of TM at home by opening with a revealing description of her house--a three story converted boathouse on the Hudson a half hour from New York City. Asked to define real beauty, TM says it is a result of a kind of

54

"repose" and "clarity about things." Anna Magnani is sexy, Marilyn Monroe is not. Writing a sexual scene, TM intends the reader to bring her/his own sexuality to the experience of the prose, so what she omits to say is crucial.

Romantic love, in its narrow sense that has evolved since WWI, seems to presuppose its own doom. In *Sula,* a rare occurrence in literature--fully realized friendship between women--was violated by Sula's sexual betrayal of her friend Nel.

Tradition is vitally important to TM. For a girl to learn to be a woman, she must know what it means to carry on the culture of "the tribe," keeping alive the connections with ancestors. She, as writer, has established a past by imagining it, and now though she speaks to a certain constituency, her work at its best is universal--as is Dickens and Beowulf. Almost as a corollary to her sense of the importance of culture, there is quick, flashing anger in TM, accusatory anger at the interviewer for being ignorant of black history, for not being curious enough about Native Americans, for not honestly confronting the past.

A cultural effect which the novelist cherishes is the interaction in black art between presenter and audience, so that something happens to that audience. That give-and-take relationship is part of black church services, of jazz music, and is potentially present in literature.

47.   Mitchell, Leatha S. "Toni Morrison, My Mother, and Me." *In The Memory and Spirit of Frances, Zora, and Lorraine: Essays and Interviews on Black Women and Writing.* Edited by Juliette Bowles. Washington, D.C.: Institute for the Arts and the Humanities, Howard University, 1979, pp. 58-60.

Deeply disturbed by TM's tendency in earlier novels to "encompass and circumscribe" her female characters on the basis of their shade of black, Mitchell resents as unrealistic the narrow categories into which the fictional figures fall. Either they are "dark-skinned (black, 'heavy-brown')" and able to "define their own existence (even if in...negative terms)," or they are "light-skinned ('lemony')...and have their existences defined by others" (p.58).

Because of their failure to reflect accurately the subtleties of black female life, TM's novels are personally unsatisfying. Two real models who loom large for Mitchell are her dark, nurturing, story-telling mother and much lighter-skinned, paternal grandmother, who raised 14 children and managed a 240 acre farm in South Carolina. Both individuals were more than caricatures, more than what the sum of their external circumstances might have made of them: both "became themselves" through conscious acts of choice. Their influences combined to help make of the author an expatriate Southerner growing up for the first 12 years of her life in Western Pennsylvania. In TM's fiction Mitchell thought to find her own unique experience (Southern heritage plus Northern upbringing) articulated, but the truth of that experience is missing from the novels. What is there is merely lifeless stuff from "an old trunk in a thrift shop...poetry, graven images, strange...individuals, surreal adventures" (p. 60).

48. Myers, Linda Buck. "Perception and Power Through Naming: Characters in Search of a Self in the Fiction of Toni Morrison." *EES* 7 (January, 1984): 39-55.

The essay makes two major observations: that there is a particular kind of power in the way that language (especially "naming") orders experience, and that TM's characters are all struggling to forge an individual identity within communal and/or social organizations. Three brief critiques--all commendatory--follow the essay.

TM's fiction is a forthright challenge to the conventional tendency to talk about experience in terms of simple oppositions such as beauty/ugliness; innocence/guilt; alive/Dead; master/servant; black/white, etc. In *TBE*, something makes the Breedlove family (especially Pecola) consider themselves ugly. The same thing (a definition of "beautiful" derived from white culture) begins to generate that feeling in the MacTeer girls, and while that "thing" remains unnamed or misnamed, the characters cannot recognize it. By the novel's close, Claudia is aware of her complicity in Pecola's tragedy. She--and other members of the black community--made themselves beautiful by accepting the insidious suggestion that Pecola was ugly, and by that complicity they make her "an Other" even as they fail in their own cases "to create a Self" (p. 42).

Sula Peace, by contrast, is independent, self-reliant, asocial, and totally engaged in the business of making a Self. Other characters can understand in a simple way the eccentricity or even the mystery of a Shadrack, and Eva, the deweys, or a Nel. They arrive at an understanding by naming the eccentricity. Yet they can never similarly understand Sula, even though they name her "roach," and "bitch," and "witch" and worse. Sula herself insists it is no simple matter to know who is good, who evil, and that difficulty of knowing or of expressing in customary language is the principle challenge to discourse raised by the book.

SOS concerns ironic naming of places (No Mercy Hospital) and misnaming of persons (Macon Dead). Milkman has to undertake a Quest for his true name, his identity, and at the novel's close he has succeeded to such an extent that "both Pilate and /he/ are free of being Dead and are flying" (p. 47). Here, then, naming gives true knowledge and even revolutionary freedom.

TB demonstrates, through the impossible love affair of Son and Jade, the unresolvable conflict "between the old values of the tribe and the new values of the city, between community and the individual, between nature and culture" (p. 49). This very open-ended work shows what is inevitably lost when one insists on an Either/Or, exclusive world view. In fact, all of Morrison's works assert language not only orders perception, but also may fossilize such perception into simplistic, dualistic systems.

49.   Nama, Charles Atangana. "Aesthetics and Ideology in African and Afro-American Fiction." Ph.D. diss., SUNY Binghamton. *DAI*. 45 (1984): 1110A

    The study identifies a critical theory with its base in African and Afro-American oral traditon and culture and then applies it to various works. TM is shown to be a precursor of the feminist aestheticians, through a detailed analysis of *TB*. With reference to theories of DuBois, Fanon, Freud, and Lacan, TM's first three novels are studied for psychoanalytical implications.

50.   Parker, Bettye J. "Complexity: Toni Morrison's Women--An Interview Essay." *Sturdy Black Bridges: Visions of Black Women in Literature*. Edited by Roseann P. Bell, Bettye J. Parker, and Beverly Gay-Scheftall. New York: Anchor Press/Doubleday, 1979, pp. 250-57.

    An interview-essay done before *SOS*, which acknowledges TM's encouragement of black work while a Random House editor, and her concentration on folk elements in her own fiction. As editor she was in charge of Henry Dumas' *Ark of Bones* and *Play Ebony Play*, as well as John McClusky's *Look What They Done To My Song* and Gayl Jones' novel *Corregidora*.

    Her motive for writing *TBE* was to show the plight of "a victim who is a child....a passive kind of person and the people around her who create the kind of situation that she is in" (p. 252).

    The author's personal version of superstition comes out in *Sula*, a book in which the relationship of certain black characters to evil was her preoccupation. She claims to have a matter of fact acceptance of the existence of evil that is characteristic of black persons and that affords them the strength of stoicism when faced with evil.

    In *Sula* TM tried to upset people's conventional understanding of "good" and "evil." Nel is the salt of the earth type, a conventionally good woman, but TM is affectionate about the disturbing Sula, as much for her living spontaneously and instinctively as for the manner in which she complements Nel: "together they could have made a wonderful single human being" (p.253). For all her offbeat values, Sula attempts briefly "to be domestic" while in love with Ajax; ironically that causes her to lose him.

    Hannah Peace is sexually promiscuous with many of her neighbors' husbands, but because she is not at all possessive, jealous, or territorial, she is not seen as a threat by the other women. In fact they like her, although she cannot quite be their "friend," and they mourn and miss her deeply when she dies.

Perhaps most puzzling is the old matriarch, Eva Peace, a character for whom "control" is important. "She is playing God. She maims people" (p. 255). Yet she is almost preternaturally observant, aware by some mysterious insight of the deep-structure similarity between her granddaughter Sula and Nel. Such a sensible, prestigious old woman deserves honor in her last days--yet she is institutionalized by the peculiarly forceful Sula. That kind of abandonment of those who have cared for us is a shameful denial of family and community responsibility.

Of black women and men, TM speaks animatedly. Her women characters and she herself face realities in their lives, and if sad realities, they cry without being bitter or whining. Women love choices, she believes, about whether to have a child or not, for instance. Black men have a choice too, and have consistently chosen not to be the fathers of the children. "I think that is called abandonment of the family or something" (p. 256). But TM also notes with some cynicism that when the white Ulysses behaved similarly, never once thinking he ought to go home to Penelope and his son, he was considered a hero!

Black women writers were not taken seriously in the past, TM says, because no women writers were taken seriously. Other kinds of creative self-expression are more accessible, more rewarding, and far less demanding of one's time.

51. Parks, Carole A. "Goodbye Black Sambo: Black Writers Forge New Images in Children's Literature." *Ebony* 28 (November, 1972): 60 ff.

Literature designed for impressionable young children shapes their thinking in pervasive ways, establishing as it does the value bases of concepts such as "pretty," "good," "family," and even of the self. Concerned that the effect of the majority of such books on black children was to make them feel excluded, authors such as June Jordan (*His Own Where*), Sharon Bell Mathis (*Brooklyn Story*), Virginia Hamilton (*The House of Dies Drear*) and others have set out to fashion experiences with language which are loving and wholesome for black readers.

Authors of materials for black children have to overcome a strong negative bias in the publishing industry, which has historically not been interested in books by black authors. Except for some work by W.E.B. Du Bois and Carter Woodson in the 1920's and a few individuals who emerged from the Harlem Renaissance in the 1930's (Langston Hughes, Countee Cullen) stereotypes dominated children's literature until the 1940's (p. 62). At that time a seminal study by librarian Charlemae Rollins (*We Build Together*) established a new, caricature-free industry standard and prompted the appearance of innovative fiction by Ellen Tarry and Jesse Jackson that featured role models appropriate to the experience of ghetto-raised youth. To this groundswell movement, biographies by Shirley Graham Du Bois were added as well as strong novels for adolescents by Lorenz Graham about rural black protagonists who were witty and capable.

Political activism of the 1960's sparked substantial reform in the policies of publishing houses. Additionally, massive infusions of financial aid to low-income school districts fueled the demand for varied, realistic and appropriate library materials. Thereafter black publishing houses such as Johnson Publishing, Drum and Spear Press, Third World Press and Broadside Press began to release books by black authors for a black public. The policy of submitting manuscripts to a black publisher is based in part on self-interest, but also and more importantly it represents the best effort of concerned writers to overcome the negative input of TV and other media today and by so doing relegate Little Black Sambo to a distant, ineffectual past.

* Pullin, Faith. "Landscapes of Reality: The Fiction of Contemporary Afro-American Women." *Black Fiction: New Studies in the Afro-American Novel Since 1945*. Cited below as item 75.

52. Saldivar, Jose David. "Claiming The Americas: Contemporary Third World Literature." Ph.D. diss., Stanford University, 1983. *DAI*. 43 (1983): 3589A.

Literature is related to cultural history, rhetoric, and ideology in the work of four authors whose writing concerns American reality in former colonial and semicolonial countries. Alejo Carpentier (*Kingdom of This World*) is studied for his use of "the theory of the marvelous." Gabriel Garcia Marquez (*One Hundred Years of Solitude*) is examined from the perspective of a Marxist deconstructionist. TM (*Sula, SOS*) provides the basis for a study of the nature of realism and marvelous realism. Everything in her narratives reflects what has happened to segments of Afro-American culture in the United States. Maxine Hong Kingston (*China Men*) combines fiction, epic, memoir, and autobiography as a means of responding artistically to racism in the United States.

53. Satterwhite, Sandra. "The Full Days of a Novelist." *NYPost* 26 January, 1974, p. 35.

Besides her career as a novelist and non-fiction writer, TM is a full time professional woman and the single parent of two boys, Ford (12) and Slade (8). After eight years of college teaching, she joined Random House as an editor specializing in the development of "a canon of black work" that features "black people talking to black people" (p. 35). Current projects include editing *The Black Book,* a collection of folk memorabilia, and the autobiography of Angela Davis.

Her own fiction treats women who exhibit a combination of toughness and tenderness. *TBE* laments the destruction of a young black girl's life because of her socially dictated obsession for that most superficial of goals, physical beauty. *Sula* concerns the problems encountered by a creative black woman who insists on living a radically free life in an era when there were no outlets for such a thing. One reviewer faulted the book for lacking the "stinging immediacy...of her nonfiction," which prompted TM's retort that glances at the autobiographical elements in the work: "She's...talking about my life. It has a stinging immediacy for me," (p. 35). *Sula* has been made a Book of The Month Club alternate selection and paperback rights have been sold to Bantam.

54.   Strouse, Jean. "Toni Morrison's Black Magic." *Newsweek* 97 (March 30, 1981): 52-57.

The lead article, designed to accompany her portrait on the cover of *Newsweek,* this piece surveys TM's life in broad biographical terms and adds a little interpretive commentary about her writing. *TBE* is discussed briefly as a fictional treatment of the theme of human abuse, and *TB* is cited as the bleakest of her portraits of an ugly America. Readers will find here little if anything about either *Sula* or *SOS*.

TM is consistently assertive about being a black writer, yet not "just" a black writer, because the so-called melting pot never worked and now we see that literature as a result is very pluralistic (p. 53). Her family's history comes out in the conversation, including the movement north from Greenville, Alabama, of her mother's family in about 1910, and her father's growing up amidst harsh racist conditions in Georgia. The maternal grandparents lost their land, so transplanted their family to Kentucky and then to Loraine, Ohio. From the family, TM learned black lore, music, language, rituals and myths, and from her schools and her own reading she picked up a love for and acquaintance with great literature.

Her own work marks a different phase in the development of black writing in America. The voices of black literture had been purely male and its subjects political, addressed to white men. TM and other women like her--some of whom she edited in her work at Random House--represent the vanguard of a new generation of black female authors. They succeed the "moral uplift" writers such as Margaret Walker, Lorraine Hansberry, Alice Childress, Gwendolyn Brooks; moreover they point a different direction from the political realists like Nikki Giovanni, Mari Evans, June Jordan, and Sonia Sanchez. TM's colleagues in the cultural awakening include Toni Cade Bambara, Alice Walker, and Gayl Jones.

TM's own college career, her marriage to and divorce from Harold Morrison, and her going into the publishing business are all sketched. From her sons and her father she learned how to imagine her way into a male character. Her work is not narrowly political. It is driven by a consistent moral vision: the need to search for an "understanding of something larger than the moment or the self" (p. 57).

55. Taylor-Guthrie, Danille. " 'And She Was Loved!': The Novels of Toni Morrison, A Black Woman's Worldview." Ph.D. diss., Brown University, 1984. *DAI.* 45 (1985): 2154-A.

The study is premised on the assertion that to critique the art of black women writers, one must know their culture. In the case of TM, comprehension of black women is more important than a knowledge of black culture at large, even though her fiction uses the language, folklore, history, and myths of the latter culture. This study creates a methodology applicable to the experience of black women and devotes a chapter to the analysis of each of TM's novels. Its conclusion is that her fiction is based on a metaphysics of love: of self, of the race as extended family, and of mankind.

56. Turner, Darwin. "Theme, Characterization, and Style in the Works of Toni Morrison." *Black Women Writers, 1950-1980.* Edited by Mari Evans. New York: Anchor Press/Doubleday, 1984, pp. 361-369.

The apparent lyricism of adolescence is presented in *TBE* as being in reality a world of incest, adultery, beatings, gossip, and pregnancy. But readers are not allowed to dismiss Cholly Breedlove nor his wife too easily for the hurt they willfully inflict on their daughter, Pecola. Each is a character with deeply human dimensions, as are all of the "grotesques" of the novel, who, though they preserve remnants of their integrity, are deformed by a kind of falseness about them.

In *Sula* the two main characters appear to be sharply contrasted, but in truth they are very similar in "their emotional isolation from other people" (p.363). The indifference they feel for others is a reflection of a general "pattern established by older family members" (p. 363). Nel and Sula lack meaningful relationships with their families, with men, and with "society about them" (pp.363-64). Both Pecola and Sula signal the presence of the scapegoat theme in TM's work: their respective communities needed these characters as a means of displacing their own guilt and fear.

In *SOS*, TM examines male friendship through a focus on Milkman and Guitar," who, like the female friends in the earlier novels, discover the superiority of intrasexual friendship over heterosexual romance (p. 366). In fact, considered on the whole, her work shows that sex is a radical basis of separation. Men can deal successfully with men, women with women, but "Black men and women--regardless of class or culture--never sustain harmonious relationships in heterosexual love" (p. 369). Milkman's search for his roots teaches him about love and community, especially the "community of Black men" (p. 366). His discovery is ironic, though, in that his great grandfather Solomon (or Shalimar) escaped slavery by flying back to Africa--so the myth says. Milkman does not recognize that he is idolizing a model who abandoned his wife and children to free himself and thus is no better than Milkman's materialistic father.

Love is rewarding for very few blacks in the arid North of this novel, and what had been hinted at in the first two books--the white oppression of blacks--is a strongly asserted theme in *SOS*. The book closes on a note of calculated ambiguity, forcing the reader to wonder: "Does the ending pessimistically affirm that flight is mere delusion, or does it affirm the theme that one may learn to fly?" (p. 368).

A "lush" style in *TBE* is made lean and vivid in *SOS*. Then TM returns in *TB* to her earlier style, with Jade, Son, Valerian, Margaret, Ondine and Sidney all being "ordinary" and even "stereotypical" characters created to illustrate the author's point about "the clash of class and culture" (p. 369).

57. White, Vernessa C. "A Comparative Study of Alienation, Identity, and The Development of Self in Afro-American and East German Fiction." Ph.D. diss,. SUNY Binghamton, 1981. *DAI*. 42(1981): 206A.

Contemporary East German and Afro-American literatures point to analagous social development in both groups, because the racial structure of the U.S. is in fact a variation of the European system of social stratification.

The work of Alice Walker and TM reveal that blacks have fallen victim to the alienation Marx warned about. The East German and American authors examined here all advocate social justice and the rights of the individual, and all concur in the belief that the desire for social justice and respect for human dignity are universally sought social ends.

58. Willis, Susan. "Eruptions of Funk: Historicizing Toni Morrison." *BALF* 16 (1982): 34-42.

An essay avowedly aiming to do something other than document the social reality of TM's fiction, this piece looks at her use of metaphor, the past in collision with the present, and at gender as ways to clarify how she treats the problem of maintaining the Afro-American cultural heritage under great psychological and environmental stress.

TM sets her novels during strategic moments in American history: *TBE* and *Sula*: the 1940's black migration to cities; *Sula*: the

1940's engagement of blacks as soldiers; *SOS*: the 1960's urban black political activism; *TB:* the 1980's and cultural exiles.

Central to TM's work is the theme of alienation, experienced in terms of losing one's cultural center, and, for women, in terms of losing their ability to "experience pleasure--orgasm or otherwise" or else their purposeful self-denial of pleasure (p. 35). Her characters resist that kind of alienation (here identified as "reification") by clinging to deeply embedded sexuality, by petty outlawry, and simply by being economically marginal. *SOS* may sound a note of liberation, but *TB* is deeply pessimistic. Characters remain stubbornly compartmentalized, black from black, black from white, and both blacks and whites from a meaningful sense of the past. Jadine is "the individual whose cultural exile is the most profound" (p.37), but individual salvation finally is unimportant. TM's deepest concern is to use characters as "epiphenomenal" and to test "the strength and continuity of the black cultural heritage as a whole" (p. 37).

Modernization is the most pernicious enemy of the black culture. Macon Dead II has been totally overwhelmed, and, in the process of accumulating wealth, is impoverished culturally. But Milkman's odyssey removes him literally from consumer society and awakens in him a sense of history together with a high degree of personal sensibility and communal, folk values.

Pilate is a singular figure in TM's work. In her case the "metaphor of lack" (she has no navel) generates a moment of self-recognition which is not racial. Pecola's lacking blue eyes, Hagar's lacking copper-colored hair, though, both produce a sense of inferiority through heightening their feelings of racial otherness. So too are bodily stigmas (Sula's birthmark) or deformities (Shadrack's "monstrous" hands) flags of demeaning social difference. Another radical technique TM uses is to present self-mutilation (Sula cutting off the tip of her finger; Eva Peace sacrificing her leg) as symbolically positive acts sharply marking the character's defiance of oppressive social norms.

All such metaphors (sexual, lack, deformity, mutilation) are calculated to disturb readers and to disrupt their having been numbed by social and/or psychological alienation (p. 40).

The most positive of the metaphors TM uses is that of a utopian, three-woman household. Her women are vigorously heterosexual, but they do not permit heterosexuality because that kind of relationship is founded on the determining principle of male dominance in working relationships (p. 41).

PART V
CRITICISM OF PARTICULAR WORKS: *THE BLUEST EYE*

59. Bakerman, Jane S. "Failures of Love: Female Initiation in the Novels of Toni Morrison." *AL* 52, no.4 (January, 1981): 541-63.

The search for love is TM's recurring theme, a theme joined to a narrative pattern which dramatizes female initiation (p. 542). Two "frames" are used in *TBE:* the primary school reader, and the family life of the MacTeers. Pecola's failed quest is highlighted by the fact that her menstruation has just begun, so when what could be healthy sexuality leads only to her rape and the death of her child, the failure of initiation is particularly poignant.

The failure is more complex in *Sula,* because in that work the individuals make many more choices which contribute to the problem. Sula and Nel are successful as young girl friends, but despite youthful achievements they cannot manage their relationship with each other or with their respective families when they are grown women.

SOS applies the initiation pattern in such a way that the reader sees some qualified successes. Pilate's initiation ultimately fails "because her family have not been able to equip her for success" and her own singularity models inadequately for her daughter Reba and granddaughter Hagar (p.556). The latter, her initiation too long delayed, enters into a sexual relationship with Milkman, but is nagged by self-doubt and is unable to sustain the relationship. Though deeply loved by her mother and grandmother, Hagar is pathetically isolated. First Corinthians Dead would appear to be an unlikely candidate to pass the female initiation test. Estranged from her father and with a mother who is herself emotionally shriveled because of failed relationships with her own father and husband, First Corinthians is surprisingly able to assert her independence from her father and to accept all the implications of her sexual relationship with Henry Porter. Consequently she accomplishes one phase of the rite of passage, but hers remains a role of total subjugation to Porter, and thus is a distinctly qualified success (p. 562).

* Bischoff, Joan. "The Novels of Toni Morrison: Studies in Thwarted Sensitivity." *SBL.* Cited above as item 32.

60. Byerman, Keith E. "Intense Behaviors: The Use of The Grotesque in *The Bluest Eye* and *Eva's Man.*" *CLAJ* 25 (1981): 447-57.

TM and Gayl Jones both resolve their respective novels by using the grotesque as a technique of social criticism. "Pecola epitomizes the American obsession with whiteness, while Eva exemplifies the society's fixation on sexual dominance" (p. 447). Features supposed normal in modern life, these novelists present as "absurd and ominous distortions" (p. 447). They attempt to reach readers beneath the usual level of consciousness and to shock them into recognition. That strategy is necessary because readers share the attitudes toward sex and race which are the objects of criticism (p.448). The use of distorted situations compels readers to consider the absurd nonrationality of social values which lead to schizophrenia, incest, and murder.

In *TBE*, whiteness is too pervasively overwhelming to be successfully resisted, hence Pecola Breedlove finally sits mad and alone in her room, babbling to herself and convinced the seer she visited will bestow on her the blue eyes that function as emblems of beauty. Even her rape by her father was motivated by his frustration and powerlessness. Readers both understand and condemn, are both attracted to the distorted characters and repulsed by them, and Pecola becomes as a result a "grotesque Messiah" sacrificed so that others of us might live with our society.

The theme and tone are different in *Eva's Man*, where Eva becomes an avenging angel, her crime a liberating horror. All women are victims in Jones's novel; the domination is sexual, frequently violent. In her own family, Eva learns that men consider women guilty even though that may merely mean being "guilty" of being attractive. Regardless of the sexual offense, despite the reality of another man's being responsible, men characteristically punish women. Theirs is a no-win predicament: protect themselves forcefully from sexual advances, and they are labeled criminal; submit and they are marked with the tag of whore. "Gender is indeed...destiny" (pp. 454-455).

In desperation, Eva strikes out, refusing to submit to her own reification. She poisons her assailant, and, after his death, bites off his penis. Grotesque though that act may be, Jones presents Eva in Christ-like terms: bleeding, with a pain in her side, imagining nails in her hands, and relating the castration to the biting of an apple (pp. 455-456). Eva's is the burden of identifying unequivocally "the true root of all evil" (p. 456).

The suffering of Pecola and Eva represent in microcosm that of all black women. The true horror, we are meant to see, is not in the fiction but in the world that fiction mirrors so truly.

61.   Christian, Barbara. "The Contemporary Fables of Toni Morrison." *Black Women Novelists, The Development of a Tradition, 1892-1976* . Westport, Connecticut and London, England: Greenwood Press, 1980, pp. 137-179.

TM's central theme--the search for beauty in a world decidedly not beautiful--is announced in her first, deceptively simple novel. Pecola Breedlove's desire for blue eyes, deemed beautiful by western standards, is a microcosmic instance of the conflict between basic Anglo-American and Afro-American cultural values ongoing in this country for generations. Speaking for the values of culturally dominant white society is a voice readers will recognize from their grade school primers. Intruding on it is the voice of Claudia MacTeer, the adolescent black girl who narrates this story about the tragic effects of the myth of beauty--even as she comprehends it well enough to resist its overwhelming her in the same way it did Pecola.

Besides the Dick-and-Jane-primer voice giving the book expansiveness, and the voice of Claudia lending it a sense of immediacy, an ironic, seasonal structure is part of the organizational scheme of the work and suggests to readers a natural movement toward love that is denied the young girls in the novel. Only cruel, hurtful, unloving things happen in the chapter entitled "Spring." Even Mrs. Breedlove's story is introduced by a flat, ironic narrative (SEEMOTHERMOTHERISVERYNICE...) and emphasizes her disillusionment in love and her unmotherly assumption that her own child is ugly, her employer's white daughter pretty. Cholly, for whom life was shaded in ugly tones when he was young, develops an ambivalent love-hate attitude toward women, and subsequently he rapes Pecola in a misconceived attempt to reconcile his conflicting feelings toward her, his wife, and even himself.

Similarity is noticeable in the stories of these individuals, because the book's total structure is circular and each chapter explores variations on a recurring, unifying theme. All the characters, for instance, are a little crazy with self-hatred of the sort that finally makes Pecola certifiable, and all of them share in the blame for her ultimate madness. Caught in the double bind of being black and female, Pecola becomes the passive scapegoat for the community.

In *Sula,* TM spins a fable about conformity and individuality. The story of staid Nel and experimental Sula is related to the survival of their community. The institution of a bizarre holiday, National Suicide Day, established by the shellshocked Shadrack, marks the sense in which the book concerns death as a major theme. Mythic suggestions in the prose are carried by metaphors of fire, water, wind, and earth, as well as by an intertwining, circular use of time, and by survivalist patterns of behavior in the women. Eva is capable of sacrificially killing her son, Plum; Hannah becomes a discriminating if voracious seeker of physical love whose death by fire dramatizes the kind and quality of her mother's love.

Most stridently "individual" is Sula. Her inquisitive behavior causes the drowning of Chicken Little; she watches her mother burn to death and makes no effort to help; she physically leaves the community for 10 years; she casually seduces her best friend's husband; she institutionalizes her grandmother. Sula's actions horrify The Bottom, making her the personification of evil in this fable. What sets her apart the most, though, is Sula's insistence on living for--on "making"--herself, not Others. That kind of total absorption is simultaneously destructive and creative in that it provides the community a common enemy, a pariah. Without such a focus for their hatred, the black community cannot like even themselves. Sula's major personal value is to Nel, although the latter does not realize it until she laments Sula's loss by the graveside.

62.   Clark, Norris. "Flying Black: Toni Morrison's *The Bluest Eye, Sula*, and S*ong of Solomon*." *MV* 4 (Fall, 1980): 51-63.

TM is committed to black art and to portraying the black American experience, but she is totally opposed to a Black Aesthetic in the narrow sense ("black is beautiful," Black Cultural Nationalism)--the type of aesthetic that became fashionable in the 60's and 70's and was espoused by Amiri Baraka, Larry Neal or Welton Smith.

As a writer, TM manages to meet the objectives of black art and also of universal art. She uses traditional archetypal forms together with black oral history, folklore and myth, sometimes overlaid with fantasy in character and setting, in order to recapture black American and black African myths and extend those myths to universal proportion. Working as she does on both the particular and mythic levels, TM creates fiction uniquely accessible and appealing to the black masses, to black intellectuals, and to both black and white litterateurs. An instance of the kind of accretion she works toward can be seen in the myth of flying. Derived in part from African culture, the myth is at once a traditional literary device of universal proportion (Icarus, Daedalus), and a localized Pageant of Birds celebrated in certain Baptist churches in Mississippi.

TM has never settled for protesting black oppression. Instead she renders the black experience in terms that make it widely understandable, generally emphasizing the black capacity to endure by maintaining emotional and spiritual strength. So real, so firmly located in black history and culture, are her Jude Greens, Cholly Breedloves and Shadracks that their fictional experiences succeed in becoming common to all people.

Black music weaves its way through her novels, giving characters a way to order their mysterious or miserable experiences and not only bear such misery but also transcend it through art. To the universally symbolic concept of the Quest, TM fuses the culturally symbolic notion of the "Negro as America's metaphor."

Thus in her novels, folk traditions associated with the cycle of seasons, with concepts of good and evil, with naming, dreams, omens, and superstitions, come to represent not just the particular lives of American blacks, but also the mythic meanings inherent in the lives of all persons.

Occasionally her work is flawed by its unusual, even inexplicable characters whose presence strikes readers as unreal, but who appear to be necessitated by the allegorical nature of her themes or by plot. In addition, the excessive goodness of her central figures, especially the women, is a flaw. Committed as she is to believing in the paramount importance of an all-accepting love, TM refuses to draw any truly bad or good characters.

63.   Dee, Ruby. "Black Family Search For Identity." *Freedomways* 11 (1971): 319-20.

A short "appreciation" piece, this note points out the book's focus on majority standards of beauty which ravage the Breedlove family. That it is fundamentally realistic is evident in the work's being "a series of painfully accurate impressions" (p. 320).

64.   de Weever, Jacqueline. "The Inverted World of Toni Morrison's *The Bluest Eye* and *Sula*." *CLAJ* 22 (1979): 402-414.

Incited by a media bombardment to conform to an impossible standard of beauty, the black woman faces a potentially maddening dilemma: to transform one's self (as in *TBE*) or to create a new self (as in *Sula*). In TM's earliest books, Pecola Breedlove goes mad trying vainly to transform herself, and Sula fails to create a self and dies. Neither the inner, psychological world nor the outer, sociological one is any help to the protagonists, because those "worlds" have been "turned upside down" (p. 403).

In *TBE*, the father violates the child, and both Breedlove parents breed hate, not love, for themselves and for others. Perverted male figures such as Mr. Henry, the roomer, and Soaphead Church form part of this inverted world as they entertain whores and fondle little girls whom they have pacified with candy or ice cream.

In *Sula* TM again uses the "inverted" theme of having negative characters cause positive reactions in people. Sula's neighbors see her as evil, but her ultimate effect on them is good. Although the novel spans 36 years with an additional 10 unaccounted for, thus allowing for more than adequate development of characters, the "why" of Sula's character remains a stubbornly unpenetrable riddle to the end. Like Eva, her grandmother, Sula amputates a piece of herself to prove her love and symbolize her courage (a similar sacrifice of one's own finger bone occurs in the Romanian folk tale, "The Enchanted Pig").

Sula always lacks a self. Her involvement in Chicken Little's death taught her she had no self, and her subsequent travels and sexual liasons failed to develop one for her. At her center is nothing but loneliness. Thus it is appropriate that she die curled in a foetal position with her finger in her mouth. Ironically Sula's final effect is good: she causes an epiphany in Nel comparable to that which occurs for Gabriel in the climax of James Joyce's story, "The Dead." Both Gabriel and Nel achieve self-awareness of the sort which promotes new life. Woman as angel is a staple of fiction by black males; woman as devil is a new creation of female writers, illustrated by Sula and Gayl Jones' Eva (*Eva's Man*).

TM's vision is bleak indeed. It suggests "the struggle..." by black girls and women "...to establish identity in a world which does not acknowledge one's existence is sometimes lost" (p. 414).

65.   Frankel, Haskel. "Toni Morrison's *The Bluest Eye*." *NYTBR* 1 November, 1970, p. 46.

TM errs in this her first novel by having "gotten lost in her construction" (p.47). The climactic episode involving Pecola's going to see Soaphead Church to ask for blue eyes occurs too late in the book to be effective. Thus the author's primary objective--to dramatize the result of race prejudice on children--is obscured by her "flights of poetic imagery" and by "fuzziness" of language, examples of which Frankel shrewdly produces. Even characters such as Frieda and Claudia can be extraneous and distracting, and so when it finally comes, Pecola's mental breakdown "...has only the impact of reportage" (p. 47).

66.   Gant, Liz. "The Bluest Eye." *BlW* 20 (May, 1971): 51-52.

Through the eyes of Claudia and Frieda MacTeer, TM forces black readers to confront "an aspect of the Black experience that many of us would rather forget, our hatred of ourselves" (p. 51). The author's technique is to show the scene, not to moralize about it, and that is "hip" and engaging of the reader's sympathy. Without the age of intelligence of Wallace Thurman's Emma Lou (*The Blacker The Berry*), Pecola Breedlove is a pathetically vulnerable object of communal derision who finally is assaulted sexually by her own father. As a consequence she slips into insanity, and the reader must ask himself seriously whether he did anything today to assist the Pecolas of the world.

67.   Hovet, Grace Ann and Barbara Lounsberry. "Flying As Symbol and Legend in Toni Morrison's *The Bluest Eye, Sula,* and *Song of Solomon*." *CLAJ* 27 (1983)): 119-40.

Symbolism of flight is used archetypally to suggest freedom or moral/spiritual ascendancy. In black cultural slave legends or in songs such as "I Got Wings," or "Swing Low Sweet Chariot," flight implies escape through death from the physical world and a return to God. In more recent social contexts, the image has been used to represent equality and opportunity (*Native Son, Sula*).

TBE emphasizes the danger of flight, particularly by examining the concept of a "fall." The Breedlove family's cat and dog both "fall" and die. Sexuality is pervasively associated with a fall. The novel uses fallen women as major figures; Pauline's teeth begin to fall out, and in her working for a bourgeoisie white family she becomes a failed version of a nesting bird--"never metamorphosing to flight" (p. 124). Cholly floats about aimlessly, indulges in flights of depravity, and finally pulls his daughter down into disintegration and spiritual death with him by sexually assaulting her.

The causes of the downfall in the novel include victimization of the black characters, but also their own negative means of coping: "safe and derivative (nesting) or...flight away from black identity and community" (p.126). Required for sustained affirmative flight is a complete sense of self plus commitment to others. In *Sula*, as in *TBE*, characters lack that, and hence plunge to their various deaths or else stagnate as failed "nesters."

Nel is a classic instance of a constricted, flightless nester, only tenuously capable of expressing "basic...grief, joy, and love" (p. 129). Sula's sexual "free falls" lead to complete isolation, and, similarly, so does Eva's life force, which is expressed negatively as hatred and confines her (except for three singular descents) to her upstairs bedroom. Only a revelation experienced by Nel late in the novel suggests the affirmative possibilities of selfhood and community.

What no character in the first two novels achieves, Milkman Dead does in the third: ascendant flight for himself plus the capacity to model affirmatively to others. He finally develops beyond indifference and possessiveness to genuine love, a centered identity, and a sense of responsibility.

By using flight imagery, TM attacks romantic myths which mislead individual characters and readers and prevent their discovering genuine self-knowledge that produces transcendence.

68. Klotman, Phyllis R. "Dick-and-Jane and the Shirley Temple Sensibility in *The Bluest Eye*." *BALF* 13 (1979): 123-125.

The essay categorizes *TBE* as belonging to the Bildungsroman tradition, a novel of growing up--in this instance as a young, black female (p.123). Basic to both structure and theme is TM's use of the primary reading book. That model establishes the ironic disparity between the imagined world of books and the real world of the home. In its most grammatically correct version, the excerpt from the primary reader evidences the "alien white world." The second version illustrates the lifestyle of the MacTeer black children, whose reality is impoverished but better than Pecola Breedlove's. The third version represents the misshapen, distorted, ruinous reality of Pecola's world. Taken together, the excerpts from the reader comprise a scathing indictment of "a society which educates--and unconscionably socializes--its young with callous disregard for the cultural richness and diversity of its people" (p. 123).

The epitome of "good, true, and beautiful" is Shirley Temple. Worshipping that model causes Pecola to be consumed by self-hatred (p.124). Unable to grow naturally into puberty, she instead withers into madness. Pecola becomes a scapegoat even for the black community, since members of it perversely view themselves as more beautiful when they see Pecola as ugly (p. 125). That the development of the story is set against a natural pattern of seasons is also designed to heighten the irony of the human desolation.

69. Lange, Bonnie Shipman. "Toni Morrison's Rainbow Code." *Crit* 24 (Spring, 1983): 173-81.

Evident in all of TM's novels and a poem for children is systematic use of color imagery to promote particular responses or sensual experiences in readers. TM's "system" is traditional and consistent: red=alarm; green=tranquillity; blue=pleasure, nurturing; white=the mystical. That systematic use of imagery is appropriate to her ends, which often are to explore traditional aspects of the past, of myth, and of folklore.

In both *TBE* and *SOS*, blue and white imagery suggests "positive, life-giving forces" or "peaceful, nonviolent" death, or even insanity when the latter is a pleasurable escape from oppressive reality (p. 175). Pecola retreats into her dream of blue eyes, Sula's death is couched in terms of blue and white imagery, and Milkman's final leap is compared explicitly to the fleetness of "a lodestar," which is blue and white.

The alarming color red is used "to increase tension and to create a feeling of foreboding in the reader" (p. 176). Some allusions are obvious (Eva's dream of a red dress the night before Hannah dies in flames; Macon Dead's fear of a voodoo doll with its belly painted red), some are only faintly suggestive (Margaret Street's red hair as evidence of a curse on her).

TM's use of green imagery connotes tranquillity, balance, and normality, as in the names of characters such as Nel Greene and William (Son) Green, or the humid "naturalness" of Valerian Street's greenhouse.

Thematic development in the author's career is also suggested by the shift from a preponderance of red imagery in the first three novels (suggesting her personal and racial frustration) to a noticeably emphatic use of yellow in *TB*. As color schemes imply, TM's latest work is the most optimistic.

Silver is used for betrayal in *TBE, SOS,* and *TB,* and gold is associated with dual and opposite images. Black too can be both positive or negative, depending on context.

70. Leonard, John. "Three First Novels on Race." *NYT* 13 November, 1970, 35.

TM's is an exquisitely crafted first novel which inquires into why beauty gets wasted in this country. "The wasting gets done by a cultural engine" (p. 35) that murders the hopes and the possibilities of black-skinned, brown-eyed young people who do not measure up to standards set by the blonde American myth. Her fiction is a moving dramatization of institutionalized waste.

71. Loftin, Elouise. "Toni Morrison's *Bluest Eye.*" *BlC.* 3 (Fall, 1971): 48.

The novel is insistently rooted in the truth of black experience. Too often and too painfully, readers will have known the self-hate of Pecola Breedlove and will understand her pathetic, consequent attempts to be special, "worthy of attention," a girl with eyes so blue "everyone would have...sit in awe and wonderment at her worth" (p.48). Because it is profoundly true, the work is certain to move readers profoundly.

72. Marvin, Patricia H. "The Bluest Eye." *LibJ* 95 (November 1, 1970): 3806.

This first novel, couched in "pungent" prose and stocked with adeptly drawn character types, is alive with insight into the childhood experience of being black. Its overall structure and its narrative flow are both weakened by "one section depicting the imaginary conversation of the now-maddened and schizoid child, delivered of a dead baby at 12," (p. 3806), but the work is of great interest to young adults and social workers.

74

73. Mickelson, Anne Z. "Winging Upward Black Women: Sarah E. Wright, Toni Morrison, Alice Walker." in *Reaching Out: Sensitivity and Order in Recent American Fiction by Women.* Metuchen, N.J. & London: Scarecrow Press, 1979, 124-53.

Literature by people considered "socially marginal" challenges traditional assumptions and communicates clearly the pain and pride in being black, a woman, and in having survived.

In *TBE* it is children who aspire, who search for that ideal which is beyond present reality. The theme is extended in *Sula*, a psychological and symbolic work built on the suggestion of a "double" in the complementary relationship between the freethinking rebel Sula and the compulsive, controlled Nel. Their actions represent a kind of "figure splitting" (p. 128) and the characters themselves function as "representations of rebel and conformist" (p. 129).

In TM's fiction, women reach out for sexual experience, and even the impulse to murder is strongly present in them--not just in men. Deaths by both water and fire figure significantly in the character development of Nel and Sula, suggesting a Dostoevsky-like theme of going beyond conventional moral strictures in order to explore the limits of one's humanity. Often the price paid for such moral exploration is one's own life--as in Sula's case. Sula may pride herself on her independence, her zest for experience, her seeing life whole and living like a tree, not "a stump," but the novel insists she is lonely and isolated in her defiance.

SOS takes the theme of individual aspiration a step farther and works it into the myth of flight. Pilate is the book's most powerful character. Her strength of self results from being in motion and in harmony with nature. More importantly, as a progenitor of Milkman and a repository of the history of black culture, Pilate helps Milkman to discover the beginnings of their family and thus to give them all a sense of renewal through a commitment to the concept of family and of name.

Gold divides Pilate from her acquisitive brother Macon, but the quest for that gold brings her together again, in the end, with Macon's son. Narrowly conceived social restrictions are not for Pilate, who cuts short her hair, becomes a bootlegger, and earns for herself the freedom afforded by economic independence. In contrast stands the character of Ruth Dead, raised in an affluent situation but now totally dependent on her husband and keeper, Macon. She has metamorphosed into a deficient woman, Macon into an unnatural man. Even his sexual preferences are twisted by an inordinate lust for material things.

Milkman's sisters, Corinthians and Lena, are lonely, demeaned women but each manages in a small way to break out of the prison of her life. Pilate's daughter Reba and granddaughter Hagar are more "natural" women but they are weak. Each is caught in a kind of sexual bondage to men. The author's feminist consciousness is evident in these narrow characterizations, but more explicitly in the contrasting character of Pilate, a genuinely free woman but one who (as in *Sula*) has to die (p. 147).

In somewhat different senses, Milkman and his friend and "double" Guitar were both maimed by childhood experience. Milkman has been trapped in a conformist environment at home and has developed the unbecoming sexual behavior of a stereotypical black male. Guitar was shaped into a murderously violent black radical by the shame and outrage he experienced over his father's death in a white-owned-and-run sawmill. Ironically Guitar becomes a stalker of his best friend, Milkman, who has been engaged in a personal odyssey that is freeing him from his father. Milkman's journey across Pennsylvania and Virginia is a picaresque type, a series of tests of soul and character, none of them fully realized.

The events of the book coalesce in a single vision: flying. Black men must "fly" from home, poverty, wives, and families. When they do, the children pay the price; the women remain earthbound. There is no absolute freedom for anyone, though, and the best limits on freedom are those the novel places on Pilate's flying "without ever leaving the ground" (p. 153): the human commitment to compassion.

74. Ogunyemi, Chikwenye Okonjo. "Order and Disorder in Toni Morrison's *The Bluest Eye*." *Crit* 19 (1977): 112-20.

TBE is a highly structured novel that deals with the lack of structure/order in the life of Pecola Breedlove in particular and of tragically oppressed blacks in racist America generally. The overall scheme of the book is announced in its first three paragraphs, which are reproductions of a passage from a primary reader. Thereafter and throughout the work, the theme is illustrated by being applied three different ways (in relation to sex, racism, and death). The same triadic pattern is evident in Morrison's use of three versions of scapegoat ritual, three types of black women, and even three black prostitutes.

The highly ordered first paragraph of the book becomes an emblem for a lie which white society foists on blacks. That which a character such as Pecola Breedlove learns from her school primer and from majority society at large has no relationship whatsoever to the grim realities of her disordered life.

TM follows the structural principles used by James Baldwin in *Go Tell It On the Mountain*. Pecola is nominally the main character (as is John for Baldwin) but she is also a "centripetal force bringing all the different characters together" (p. 114). She is woven through the plot and provides a focus for the theme of the scapegoat, but her madness is somewhat mechanically motivated. Ogunyemi believes TM has borrowed sociological notions from Hernton's *Sex and Racism in America* without adequately transforming them into fiction.

75. Pullin, Faith. "Landscapes of Reality: The Fiction of Contemporary Afro-American Women." in *Black Fiction: New Studies in the Afro-American Novel Since 1945*. Edited by A. Robert Lee. New York: Barnes and Noble, 1980, pp. 173-203.

Contemporary writing by black women is rooted in the cultural nationalism and feminism of Zora Neale Hurston, whose work as a folklorist and anthropologist was dedicated to articulating the innovative and creative contribution to American life made by black culture. Particularly difficult is the task of cutting through prevailing myths about black women (cf. Michele Wallace, "Black Macho and the Myth of the Superwoman," *Ms*, January, 1979).

Nella Larsen's protagonist Helga Crane (*Quicksand*, 1928) is overcome by her own self-destructive anger and despair, but protagonists of fiction by both Gayl Jones and TM, stimulated by the promise of radical change in the 1960's, work extremely hard and with notable success to establish themselves as active figures, fighters in their respective worlds.

"The task of the contemporary black female writer is to resist imposed definitions" (p. 180) and provide new information for readers to assess more accurately the experience of black women. The writers' denial of socially determined, stereotypical roles is typified in original, offbeat accounts of their own sexuality, of being women who suffer breakdowns, who are perhaps unfaithful, or single and alone, or humiliated by divorce, or who may even abuse or neglect their children. Alice Walker's collection, *In Love and Trouble* (1973), and Mary Helen Washington's edition of *Black-Eyed Susans* (1975) stand as proof texts of a black feminist movement, the "manifesto" for which was stated in Walker's article in *Ms* magazine in May, 1974, and which has as its goal a neo-realistic representation of their artistic condition.

One trauma unique to black women is the challenge posed to one's sense of self by the shade of the skin and/or type of hair. In TM's *TBE*, Pecola Breedlove's sense of self-esteem is irretrievably lost when she accepts as proper and desirable a white standard of beauty that is for her forever unattainable. The young girl is not unique in her despair. Pauline, her mother, is similarly seduced by the movies into believing in and searching for the destructive "ideals" of romantic love and physical beauty. When she is necessarily disappointed in her search, having as she does to deal with harsh and demeaning reality in her despairing, abusive husband, Cholly, Pauline begins thoughtlessly to punish Cholly and maltreat her daughter. Trapped as they are in a vicious cycle of rejection and anger, the Breedloves are fated for destruction. Pecola is at the end hopelessly mad, but the community recognizes to some extent the scapegoat function she served for them, and the reader is fully aware of the humanity and compassion of the book's presentation of the deepest psychic fears of black women.

Sula (1973) treats the ambivalent relationship between an autonomous black woman and the black community whose predetermined roles and norms she violates. The novel forces readers to reassess even the meaning of basic concepts of love. Sula finds sex but never comradely love with a man. Both she and Nel discover "a lover was not a comrade and never could be--for a woman" (p. 196). Mothers speak of "loving" their children but not liking them, and Sula herself lectures Jude about the "love" (envy) other people feel for black men (p. 197).

Experimental, disturbing, threatening to the existing order, Sula Peace is TM's instrument for pointing out new approaches to social, sexual, and psychological reality. In her is announced the theme carried forward by Alice Walker's protagonist in *Meridian* (1976), and by Gayl Jones's more sensational subject matter in *Corregidora* (1975), *Eva's Man* (1976), and the stories that comprise *White Rat* (1977). That theme is further enriched by the short fiction of Toni Cade Bambara, and the autobiographical writing of Maya Angelou and Louise Meriwether.

76. Royster, Philip M. "The Bluest Eye." *FW* (Winter, 1977): 35-44.
     The novel is focused on the problems of society's scapegoats such as Pecola Breedlove, raped by her father and rejected by her mother, and on the persona of the narrator, Claudia MacTeer, who comes to understand her own part in the scapegoating process.
     Strengths of the work include its engaging, imaginative prose, chapters constructed like essays of ideas, a captivating collection of female figures, and an impressive sense of history and sociological reality. Assets outweigh liabilities, but the work is flawed by the failure of the narrator-persona to recognize the strength of her own development--through pain--into adulthood.
     Central to the book is the theme of beauty. Based as the standard is on white American stereotypes, it has a devastating effect on the sense of self-worth of any character who does not conform. Pecola wants so badly to be identifiably lovely (and loved) that she begins to fantasize about herself in increasingly destructive ways. Related to "the bluest eye" aesthetic is the mulatto aesthetic, according to which those blacks are considered most beautiful who most closely resemble whites. Maureen Peal is, by this measure, an American

beauty, a "high yellow dream child," (p. 37) yet she is simultaneously a scapegoat-victim.

So too are Geraldine and her son, Louis Junior, complementary characters who functionally dramatize the theme of self-hatred and hatred of others. Geraldine has been alienated from her Afro-American culture and, in her passion to rise socially, to be "colored" instead of "nigger," has learned to despise her own historical roots. Thus she loses touch with a vitalizing "funkiness" and what it means to be truly alive. Louis Junior hates his mother as a consequence, but directs his anger at helpless cats and young black girls. Soaphead Wilson, another of TM's variations on the role of middle class mulatto persecutors of Pecola, is a particularly deceptive type of misogynist, his generalized hatred a consequence of his historical lineage, its attendant Anglophilia, plus his own repeated failure to attain any of the successes (becoming priest, psychiatrist, social worker, minister) which his mulatto ancestry might have afforded. He only appears to help Pecola realize her heartfelt wish for blue eyes; in fact he is a child molester, a victimizer of her innocence as surely as was her father.

Most directly liable for the scapegoating of Pecola are her own parents. On the one hand, Polly has herself been victimized by the destructive notions of beauty and romantic love promoted by Hollywood. That she cannot actualize her ideals makes her bitterly disillusioned and causes her to turn against her children. On the other hand, Cholly has been battered by abandonment both before his birth and again at age 14 when he tries unsuccessfully to claim his father as parent. The "freedom" he learns from never having been parented is corrosively egotistical, and he becomes in the novel the paradigm of the banished scapegoat who survives, but whose existence is mere despair (p. 41).

One's judgment of the novel rests finally on one's assessment of its main character, the narrator, Claudia MacTeer. Out of Claudia's narrative awareness both of environmental causes for Pecola's madness and of Claudia's own role in her friend's destruction should come hope of the sort that is generated by human recognition and acceptance of responsibility. But as the reader stands outside the work and evaluates Claudia's awareness, it becomes evident that she has not developed the kind of insight on which a genuinely affirmative reading can be based. Claudia unfortunately remains childishly naive in her assumptions about seasonal control over the fate of characters, and she is too resigned to the notion that resisting the destructive forces in our environments (social and psychological) is impossible.

77. Sissman, L.E. "Beginner's Luck." *NYorker* 46 (January 23, 1971): 92-94.

The reviewer laments the economics of publication and the egoism of reviewing which together militate against first novels ever reaching print, or, if they do survive thus far, of being noticed by reviewers.

Two first novels, William Crawford Woods' *The Killing Zone*, and TM's *The Bluest Eye* are among the most morally meaningful and deeply knowledgeable books this reviewer has ever seen. They concern themselves with subcultures of great significance: the military and the black family. Morrison's specific subject is black children, and she portrays them and their unrealizable dreams of glory derived from the ideals of white society, together with their appallingly oppressed parents, with stunning accuracy and emotional power.

By fictionalizing with such credibility the dismal effects on characters who come to believe that being black means being ugly, TM vividly demonstrates to her readers the necessity for the overcompensatory movement that coined the phrase " Black is beautiful."

Framing her story within the words of a white elementary school reader is an unnecessary irony, and occasionally her prose becomes "false or bombastic" (p.94). One the whole, though, the book is both true and promising.

78. Sokolov, Raymond A. "The Bluest Eye." *Newsweek* 30 November, 1970, pp. 95-96.

Contrary to much black writing which sounds like political harangue to "frighten whites...and to cajole or exhort...blacks into...revolution" (p. 95), TM's lyrical novel about growing up black sounds more like a conversation. Her prose is convincing and commanding; her story recounts the melancholy decay of one young black girl whose impossible dream is for blue eyes and whose realities drive her mad.

79. "The Bluest Eye." *Booklist* 67 (May, 1971): 729.

Perceptive dialogue combined with realistic situations here produce an important sociological novel. The emotions of black girls entering adolescence, the blighted dreams of parents drawn by false hopes to the city, an incestuous assault and the psychic harm it inflicts--these harsh elements make TM's first novel compelling indeed.

80. "The Bluest Eye." *Choice* 8 (October, 1971): 1018.

Motivated by the hatred of oppression that has inspired other contemporary black authors, TM creates a moving, sympathetic portrait, reminiscent of Richard Wright's *Black Boy* (1945). This, however, involves a young black girl overwhelmed and destroyed by a web of prejudice. The novel is cliched in both style and content, but deserves to be read.

81.   "The Bluest Eye." *KR* 38 (September 15, 1970): 1058.
      Skillfully TM forces the reader to become aware of the poignant small tragedy that happens all around us but is generally unseen ("the fall of a sparrow for whose small tragedy there was no watching eye"). Pecola Breedlove cannot thrive in the environment where she is planted, because it values blue-eyed, white-skinned Shirley Temple-types, and Pecola is black, ugly (so she believes), and loveless. Rejected by her mother, raped by her father, Pecola bears a stillborn child and in despair clutches at a last, impossible hope: that she might be given blue eyes by a local faith healer. Inevitably she "inches over into madness" (p. 1058).

82.   "The Bluest Eye." *Publisher's Weekly* 24 August, 1970, p.45.
      The unbearable plight of being poor, black, defenseless, and ugly (even in the eyes of other poor blacks) is Pecola Breedlove's burden. She is finally driven into insanity by it. Morrison writes with great compassion and with realism about the "emotional and physical poverty of black life in middle America" (p. 45).

83.   Wilder, Charles M.   "Novels By Two Friends." *CLAJ*   15 (December, 1971): 253-55.
      Both racism and savage family problems (an embittered mother, an alcoholic and perhaps insane father) beset Pecola Breedlove. Her eventual madness is a result of the concrete causes of being raped by her father and bearing his stillborn child, plus the more abstract cause of never having "had any control whatever over the outcome of her life" (p. 254). She was doomed before she was conceived.
      Wilder believes it a matter of praise (rather than a flaw) that Pecola's predicament can be seen as not exclusively the result of being poor and black, because that makes it universal.

PART V
CRITICISM OF PARTICULAR WORKS: *SULA*

* Bakerman, Jane. "Failures of Love: Female Initiation in the Novels of Toni Morrison." *AL*. Cited above as item 59.

* Bischoff, Joan. "The Novels of Toni Morrison: Studies in Thwarted Sensitivity." *SBL*. Cited above as item 32.

84. Blackburn, Sara. "Sula." *NYTBR* 30 December, 1973, p. 3.
    TM is marvelously skillful, her fiction reminiscent of that of Gabriel Garcia Marquez. Yet ultimately her concerns are still narrow and even provincial. If she is to earn a reputation as something more than a "black woman writer," she must broaden her concerns for riskier contemporary reality than the "beautiful but. . . distanced novel" (p. 3) such as she has produced in *Sula*.

85. Bragg, Melvin. "Black Bottom, U.S.A." *Punch* 279 (November 5, 1980): 826.
    America's polyglot culture has provided the material for a number of fictional forays into new "countries." TM's *Sula* is an excursion into another such. Hers is a black culture, "Faulkner turned inside out" (p. 826) or a black version of Steinbeck's Cannery Row legends. She initiates the reader into a secret society which has greatly enriched both black and white people, and she admonishes us to treasure that culture, which she suggests contains the essential artistic wealth of America.
    Blacks "digested the American experience and turned it into art," (p.826), and TM similarly draws from within herself and spins into insightful art the experience of black eccentrics and scheming, murderous, loving mothers, and disturbingly independent women, and a frightened, hostile community. All three of her novels, but especially her best work in *Sula*, comprise a new vision of "America's understanding of itself" (p. 826).

86. Bryant, J.H. "Something Ominous Here." *Nat* 219 (July 6, 1974): 23-24.
    Significant works of recent black literature have focused with unnerving consistency and chilling detachment on the fact of evil in the psyche of the major characters. Without being willing to call the appearance of such works a "movement," Bryant is disturbed by a cool preoccupation with brutality in the fiction of Ed Bullins, Alice Walker, and TM (*Sula*).

When she deals with the too easily satirized fact of white prejudice or petty black bourgeoisie, TM is not in any sense original. But when she shapes a Sula, the author is working creatively and powerfully, even if in a vein which threatens to become amoral.

* Christian, Barbara. "The Contemporary Fables of Toni Morrison." *Black Women Novelists, The Development of a Tradition, 1892-1976*. Cited above as item 61.

* Clark, Norris. "Flying Black: Toni Morrison's *The Bluest Eye, Sula,* and *Song of Solomon.*" *MV*. Cited above as item 62.

87. Croswell, Elva L. "Woman As Artist In The Novels of Colette, Anais Nin, and Toni Morrison." Ph.D. diss., University of Southern California, 1985. *DAI* 46 (1985): 417-A.
    Using Colette's *La Vagabonde,* Anais Nin's *A Spy In The House of Love* and "Elena," and TM's *Sula,* the study analyzes the quest for self-fulfillment in iconoclastic, creative women. Colette deals with the dilemma of women living alone, Anais Nin with the need to be sexually fulfilled, and TM with the effect of American society on black women.

88. Davis, Faith. "Sula." *HarAdv* 107, #4 (Special Issue, 1974): 61-62.
    Sula is an "engaging and illuminating book about pain and estrangement" (p.61) as those devastating emotions shape the lives of the black community in the Bottom. There the citizens may seem at a glance to be entirely ordinary, but the fiction shows us their complexity and their ability to endure under staggering burdens. The quality of engagement which readers experience through the book is a result of TM's lyrical yet spare and visionary language.

89. Fisher, Jerilyn. "From Under the Yoke of Race and Sex: Black and Chicano Women's Fiction of the Seventies." *MV* 2 (Fall, 1978): 1-12.
    Fiction by Estela Portillo, TM, Alice Walker, Gayl Jones, and Toni Cade Bambara is representative of a new genre: literature of women, by women, and focused on characteristic dilemmas of minority females. The genre reveals a new approach to racial identity and to the problems of being persecuted on the basis of race and/or sex.
    Most minority women, engrossed in traditional family roles, exercise power and influence at home, but always in a role subordinate to the male who presumes her frailty and shields her. All the women characters in *SOS,* for instance, except Pilate are pitiable

in their tacit assent to the notion of female subordination. The Dead women are monied and genteel; working class black women face a different predicament. The labor they perform out of necessity puts them in direct competition with men, and so either they must usurp male prerogatives or abandon traditional female responsibility. Lower class females in literature by Chicano women usually choose to stay with the provincial mores, because although men have the "right" to rule, women have an informal power as strong mothers which makes them the center of the household and the guarantors of community survival.

That same submissive behavior by a woman in black literature would not earn respect for the character. There it is through force and aggression (not obedience to patriarchal law) that black mothers wield power.

Among the most inhibiting of conditions for minority women is sex. Nearly all the female characters are sexually or emotionally abused. In fact men and women continually victimize one another, and as a consequence of the domestic exploitation there are no long-lasting, male-female relationships. The poisoning and castration that marks Gayl Jones' *Eva's Man,* the sexual abuse at the center of TM's *TBE,* the woman's malicious revenge in Portillo's "The Trees,"--all these abuses are fictional instances of truths that mirror social reality. When men and women are defenseless victims of racial prejudice which incites sexual exploitation, they use each other as "releases" for their own anger. Thus violence and cruelty of a unique, intimate sort become recurring themes of minority fiction by women.

A way for women to counter the effects of male dominance is to establish meaningful relations with other women. Rosalie Peralta's "The Two Sisters" illustrates such sisterhood at work, as does Portillo's "The Paris Gown." In *SOS*, Pilate, Reba, and Hagar make up a uniquely knit female group. And in some recent fiction homosexual love is advocated and women characters enter into relationships that categorically exclude men.

With increasing frequency, fiction by minority women sounds a note of exhortation to its readers. Writers do not show characters who achieve happiness by acquiescence to traditions that smother a woman's singularity. Instead "maverick" characters like Sula, Pilate, Josefa (*Day of The Swallows*), and others function to incite readers to be more audacious in evaluating their aspirations. The net effect of this genre of fiction is to make many readers want to join the battle against sexual oppression and for greater self-determination.

There is in the Black Power movement an implicit conflict between history and change. In their drive to discover their roots, modern blacks find themselves struggling to free themselves from their history of enslavement. The Chicano political struggle on the contrary, is less divisive. It is concerned with maintaining its heritage, and one consequence of that is to focus the attention of the Chicano community on resisting full assimilation into white society in

86

a way that would obscure the Mexican-American identity. Mother-daughter conflict in fiction illustrates a difference in the two ethnic struggles: revolutionary Chicano daughters do not slight the traditional role of the mother, and whereas Chicano mothers gain power through submission, black mothers do so by being overtly commanding.

90. Francis, William A.C. "Sula." *Best Sellers* 33 (January 15, 1974): 469.

Sula is especially disappointing because second novels are examined more closely for evidence of a writer's staying power and durability than first books. That evidence is not present in the chaotic, incredible narrative of *Sula*. Minor characters are either grotesque or stereotypical. Sula herself is one dimensional, her evil power over the black community unexplained, her malevolence to her family and disruptive effect on her best friend's marriage unmotivated and incomprehensible to an audience.

91. Grumbach, Doris. "Fine Print." *NRep* 9 March, 1974, p. 31.

TM's second novel is a poetic, touching study of the lives of two black women, one of whom appears initially to have escaped the confines of her poor life in a small community whereas the other stays put and endures. The book is well-written and believable.

TM also edited *The Black Book*, a collection of memorabilia pertinent to the history of blacks in America, and designed for a nonscholarly readership. Its theme is "the survival and endurance of blacks despite everything" (p. 31).

92. Hollinghurst, Alan. "Making Up." *NS* 100 (November 28, 1980): 24.

TM takes a calculated risk in her second book (an elegy on the passing of "the bad old times," p. 24) in that it is identifiably a "reissue" of her first. Her evocative writing makes *Sula* successful, despite relying heavily on fictive shortcuts (creating characters already familiar as types) and despite her central figure's remaining "mysteriously insubstantial" and her coloring with sentimentality events which are explicitly disturbing.

93. Jefferson, Margo. "Toni Morrison: Passionate and Precise." *Ms* 3 (December, 1974): 34-38.

Those who operate from traditional biases and claim that blacks, Jews, and women cannot produce great art are conclusively rebutted by TM's first two novels. The bigot's assumption is that their very oppression makes the black, Jew, or woman incapable of achieving the kind of distanced objectivity great art demands.

TBE and *Sula* are both couched in language which is "passionate and precise; lyrical and philosophical" (p.34). Their informing perspective is sexual, but that is a subtle variety of unconscious sexuality of the sort which feels no need to argue for or protest against the presence of "the man."

Like a musician, TM interweaves tones, textures, and emotional balances, playing scenes of the ordinary and commonplace (first menstruation) against the profound and rare (a close, personal acquaintance with death). In *TBE* the fragile psyche of a young black girl is crushed before it has any chance to develop. In *Sula*, the two 12 year old girls (bonded by a terrible secret of shared responsibility for death) have to grow up and apart. Nel and Sula are distinct and take distinctly different paths to adulthood. Yet they are never truly estranged, and in fact a rupture in their relationship caused by Sula's carelessly sleeping with Nel's husband Jude is repaired, and they are physically together before Sula dies. This bare, necessary reliance on each other is TM's strategy for showing in a microcosmic way the larger truth about black women: they "always had friends--because they didn't have anybody else" (p. 37).

The informed perspective which knowledgeable readers have of the author's technique is occasionally shared by especially insightful characters. Sula sees herself as a microcosmic "type": as she is dying, so too is every colored woman in this country, she says. Her life has been different from theirs, she claims with some arrogance, because it was singular, magnificent--if only in its having been uniquely hers.

Small features of TM's books, images such as "Nuns go by as quiet as lust...," are among the wonders of the work which this reviewer appreciates.

*   Lange, Bonnie Shipman, "Toni Morrison's Rainbow Code." *Crit.* Cited above as item 69.

94.   Lehmann-Haupt, Christopher. "Underwritten and Overwritten." *NYT* 7 January, 1974, p. 29.

Although the reader vaguely intuits TM's intention in *Sula*, that intention is never realized. Her evocative recreation of a black community, her poignant sketching of the violence with which her characters live, her gripping portrait of Sula ("American fiction's first female 'bad nigger'--that scapegoat that speaks in its defiant death of the uncreated anger of its race," p. 29), such fictional elements appear to promise novelistic cogency. Yet ultimately they remain disparate pieces. Even her distinctive, poetic language seems finally to break up the narrative and also to betray her failure to sufficiently objectify highly autobiographical material so as to make it successful fiction.

95.   Lounsberry, Barbara and Grace Ann Hovert. "Principles of Perception in Toni Morrison's Sula." *BALF* 13 (1979): 126-29.

TM's novel spotlights the inherent conflict in attempting to cling to traditions of the past while adopting progressive values of the present and future. Helene Wright tries unsuccessfully to insulate herself from her past represented by her notorious mother. Then daughter Nel ultimately reverts (after a liberating adolescence spent with Sula) to her mother's repressive middle class morality (p. 126). Eva Peace sustains herself with hate, but her granddaughter Sula manages to have the idiosyncratic old woman put into a home anyway.

Thus TM can be seen to be unremittingly critical of the inclination of the people of the Bottom to turn inward in an attempt to protect themselves from the world. Sula alone among them remains independent, free and adventuresome--not committed to any single principle of order (p. 128). But hers is a shockingly new type of female reality which neither the Bottom nor the outside world can accept nor change. So in all honesty, TM admits that the "multiple perspective" variety of freedom represented by Sula has its own severe limitations. The author refuses to provide any pat answer to the agonizing question of how to reconcile the old and the new (p. 129).

96.   Martin, Odette C. "Sula." *FW* (Winter, 1977): 35-44.

The essay seeks to determine the literary function of *Sula* and to assess the accuracy of the aesthetic judgments made by Addison Gayle ("Blueprint For Black Criticism," *First World*. Jan, Feb, 1977) of recent black fiction generally and of TM's novel in particular.

In 1926, Langston Hughes promoted a set of "special Negritude" literary conventions. In effect, *Sula* is a critique of those conventions because their outcome is to foster a dangerously self-centered ethnocentrism which encourages survival values for blacks (whether those values are functional or not). Furthermore those conventions tend to affirm the sexual, natural aspects of life "to the detriment of needed rational and pragmatic strategies" (p. 35). TM's aesthetic, like that of Gayle, is one which says black art must promote the well being of the black community. Yet she differs from Gayle in that her method involves using negative images of black life in order to represent the whole truth of the group's experience. Gayle, on the contrary, considers such negative images or symbols to be stereotypical and pathological and hence capable only of worsening the black situation.

Shadrack is TM's metaphor for the "new Negro" of the Harlem Renaissance. Although he is a prototype of the freed slave, he is securely bound by a psychosis that renders him ineffectual (fear of his hands). He becomes an unbalanced, "headless" body espousing National Suicide Day. His character points to the critical judgment that the guiding principle of the black ethos is its failure to be holistic. Its view of life is too fragmented. Rationality is omitted, and the characters thus come to believe the only response to evil is to endure it. By thoughtlessly accepting their powerlessness, they in effect institutionalize helplessness, hence coming to celebrate evil as good--a special Negritude literary convention.

Even the much admired female figures of the novel, Eva, Hannah, and Sula Peace, are special Negritude images of fundamental powerlessness. Eva stands for survival, for life (regardless of quality) at any cost. Hannah images the natural, primitive life of easy sexuality, whereas Sula is merely a more sophisticated version of that. Totally self-centered, she appropriates a type of male freedom and lives a supposedly free, sensory existence.

Besides using her characters as a means of criticizing Negritude values, TM also creates, by means of presenting a whole spectrum of conventional "types," "a full fledged allegory of Black literary history" (p.38). From that history the "Tragic Mulatto convention," "Black Arts of the Sixties," "Black mother/son conventions," the "Folk trend," the "Primitive and Exotic," the "Harlem Renaissance," the "New Negro literature"--all can be found emblematically in characters and/or incidents of the book.

In Eva's blurring of the potentially distinct personalities of the deweys, TM satirizes what should be a positive concept of a sense of kinship in the Afro-American family. Another distortion in black life occurs in the traditional definition of womanhood as lacking "all freedom or triumph" (p.40). The friendship between Nel and Sula, comments on the old dichotomy between head and heart, and by bringing their friendship into conflict with heterosexual love, TM communicates her belief about the destructiveness of romantic love, which all too typically becomes "possessive mating" (p. 40).That she recognizes the importance of black sisterhood is clear from TM's insistence that "simple caring for" another is more important than sex.

Sula's function in the novel is to critique black values and behaviors. Her doing so points readers to her identity: she is "potential: the raw energy of Life and the creative impulse of Art" (p. 41). But both life and art require a purposeful end as well as experimental drive. That end is "the betterment of man and his universe" (p. 41), which can be realized only by disciplining the self. Shadrack, having lost his "head" and hidden his hands sees just death, not betterment, as an end. Sula, the Exotic, dies of cancer (literally self-destruction), while Eva, the Folk Woman, ends her life in an old people's home. Sula is, on the whole, a stern call to readers to reject the suicidal powerlessness that derives from the ethos of submission: "Ain't nothin' I can do about it" (p. 42).

In addition, the novel testifies to the need for art to make life more meaningful and beautiful. TM's method, though, is a departure from the aesthetic outlined by critic Gale. She portrays black life with all of its weaknesses as well as strengths. Stereotypes, negative images, pathology--all appear in her fiction because within them exists a hard kernel of sociological reality that must be confronted. TM implies "that constructive self-criticism is the best, perhaps the only, way to ensure that we also confront white racism directly" (p. 44). Hence this author's first priority is to critically, honestly, truthfully examine all aspects of the black ethos and the black way "of viewing the world" (p. 44).

97   Marvin, Patricia. "Sula." *LibJ* 98 (August, 1973): 2336.

Couched in terms of a lifelong friendship between two young black women, the experience of an entire black community during a 40 year period is here evocatively recreated. Nel's life is a model of normalcy: she remains in the community, marries, and has a family. Sula launches herself with gusto into the world at large and returns to disrupt nearly all the settled sexual and social mores of the folks in the Bottom. To them, she becomes evil incarnate. Only her friend Nel grieves at Sula's death.

The prose has TM's rare gift for authenticity.

98.   McClain, Ruth R. "Toni Morrison's Sula." *BlW* 23 (June, 1974): 51-53. *Sula* is a veritable taste treat for readers, its wide variety of characters as delicious as Baskin Robbins' ice cream. Its women figures are admirable, its men desirable. The folklore and symbolism provide a kind of pleasure that lasts after the reading is finished.

*   Mickelson, Anne. "Winging Upward Black Women: Sarah E. Wright, Toni Morrison, Alice Walker." *Reaching Out: Sensitivity and Order in Recent American Fiction by Women.* Cited above as item 73.

99.   Miller, Adam. "Breedlove, Peace and the Dead: Some Observations on the World of Toni Morrison," *BlSch* 9 (March, 1978): 47-50.

The fictive "world" of TM blends the best of received information from parents and grandparents, plus education in European and American literature, along with her own lived experience as a professional woman and mother. The towns she creates are small and northern, her characters almost exclusively black (the whites a mere "necessary evil," p. 48), provocatively and suggestively named, and possessed of great social and spiritual dignity as well as deep, certain self-knowledge if they are the older generation. Those positive attributes are severely "diluted" in younger, more modern figures. Ancestral characters who were not broken, who survived oppression and built successful, creative lives from their meager lots, become exemplary role models in TM's fiction. Love, for instance, is epitomized in the actions of Pilate and stern, unrelenting Eva Peace, just as surely as it is missing from the behavior, the being, of perverted Cholly Breedlove and even (for most of his life) Milkman Dead.

TM is preoccupied by the harmfulness of a notion such as "beauty," and she returns time and again to metaphors of flight (for aspiration) as well as to explicit religious concepts such as guilt, redemption, and sanctification (see especially *TBE*). In her love of and ability to manipulate language (riddle, paradox, irony), she is Joycean. And always she confounds readers with her vision of life's diversity, of its illusory, multiple, and conflicting truths.

100. Munro, C. Lynn. "The Tattooed Heart and The Serpentine Eye: Morrison's Choice of An Epigraph for *Sula*." *BALF* 18 (1984): 150-54.

TM borrows the following quote from Tennessee Williams' *The Rose Tattoo:* "Nobody knew my rose of the world but me....I had too much glory. They don't want glory like that in nobody's heart" (*Three By Tennessee*. New York: New American Library, 1976, p. 199).

The epigraph signals *Sula*'s theme and the fact that the play and novel are analogues to be read consecutively. Both Serafina Delle Rose and Sula cling to a solipsistic world view that justifies the selfish lives they live, and at the same time leaves them paralzyed in a state of self-immolation. Because of differences between drama's live performance immediacy and the distance between fiction and its audience, TM is less restricted. She can construct a detailed, ironic context which allows readers to see Sula as being like the residents of Medallion in attempting to shape a life in a white world without compromising herself (p. 150). Both Williams and TM undercut reader expectation about who is good and evil in order to force the audience to engage the work more deeply.

Serafina loses her husband, Rosario, and being without a center, she ritualistically devotes herself to a life that has ended. She cannot respond meaningfully to her daughter Rosa, and the religious rituals she maintains are evidently empty gestures. In *Sula*, it is Nel who cannot deal positively with the loss of her husband, Jude. She withdraws when she discovers him making love to Sula, first retreating to her bathroom, then more psychologically by repressing a "grey ball...of fur and string and hair always floating in the light near her" (p. 109). The grey ball is a welter of emotion which Nel stubbornly refuses to untangle until the novel's end.

Sula can be easily seen to be a part of Nel, the part that makes her capable of independent judgement. When she rejects Sula, Nel surrenders that quality and becomes the unquestioning, conventional community (p. 152). Nel and Serafina are both hurt women who become overbearing mothers as they try to transfer their love to their children. Each finally develops a tenuous kind of increased understanding of the difference between love that nurtures and love that constricts (p. 152). For TM, the positive model is found in the love between women (Nel and Sula), the negative, dependent model in the main heterosexual relationship (Nel and Jude). Sula insists on pursuing totally selfish, alternative realities. She admits no obligations or commitments to anyone other than herself and as a consequence is labeled evil by the community to which she returns at the end of her life. What she sees as nurturing her soul, in reality can be said to have starved it (p. 153) of critically necessary human contact.

In psychological terms, the novel concerns the dangers of love as possession, which this culture teaches especially to men and somewhat less forcefully to women. To express love is to accept the other as an independent self and to allow that other to be/do what he/she must (p. 154).

101.   Naughton, John. "Empty Houses." *List* 100 (November 20, 1980): 700-01.

This second novel spans more than 20 years in the life of two black girls and the community they grow up in. It is distinguished by the author's "amazing gift for dialogue" (p. 701). One of the girls becomes an extremely disruptive force in the marriages and social order of the community and finally dies "a pariah" (p. 701).

102.   O'Connor, Douglas. "Sula." *BIC Annual* 6 (1974-75): 65-66.

Black women and black love are the themes of *Sula,* and TM dramatizes both strikingly in this tale, couching her unforgettable characters and starkly truthful narrative in dazzling language.

Different types of love are shown in the examples of Eva (tough, sacrificial mother love), in Hannah (casually necessary but nonpossessive physicality), in Nel (conventional possessiveness), and in Sula (egotistical, unaccommodating sensuality). Her book concerns the "shape...futility...and pain" (p. 66) of love in a world in which women are the decision makers and "men are either weak or mad" (p. 66).

103. Ogunyemi, Chikwenye Okonjo. "Sula: 'A Nigger Joke.' " *BALF* 13 (1979): 130-33.

Sula is an attempt to show readers how wit and humor can meet the needs of people whose dreams are deferred perpetually. The whole book is an ironic tale which provokes reader awareness while offering "comfort through laughter" (p.130).

Sula becomes a scapegoat for the Bottom even as she is an unwilling catalyst for good in the community. She and Nel are complementary figures, in their views of responsibility, and morality, and sexuality. To extend the sense of "a nigger joke," one should see that Nel, although assumed by the townspeople to be a heroine, is actually the villain (p. 131).

The names of places (the Bottom, Medallion) and of characters (Shadrack, Plum Peace, Eva, Dewey) all have emblematic significance. Structurally, the book is circular, like a medallion. Thematically it concerns the position of black women in society (p. 132) and draws the men in very unflattering terms (p. 133). Rigorous in her honesty, TM looks inward with this book, and sees black life as being sometimes imitative and artificial (p.133).

No narrowly conceived work, the novel is finally about "us all" and for us all, because "nigger jokes are not only told by blacks for blacks but can also be told by anybody to anybody for comfort when the world has gone awry" (p.133).

104. Ordonez, Elizabeth J. "Narrative Texts By Ethnic Women: Rereading The Past, Reshaping The Future." *MELUS* 9 (Winter, 1982): 19-28.

The essay is a comparative study of the narratives of TM's *Sula*, Estela Portillo's *Rain of Scorpions*, Maxine Hong Kingston's *Woman Warrior*, and E.M. Broners *Her Mothers* for the sense in which those selections reshape female history, myth, and identity by getting past "cultural nationalism." Kingston blends autobiographical recollection with her own original versions of folklore and myth so as to engage the reader in "revising" the Chinese-American past. Broner's work uses Jewish traditions and is structured as a journey. Her protagonist searches for her own lost daughter and simultaneously researches a text on 19th century American women such as Louisa May Alcott and Emily Dickinson. The text's satiric thrust forces readers to revise "traditional, male-defined notions of women in history" (p. 21).

Instead of claiming the authority of patriarchal texts (the Bible, traditional myths), Sula establishes the authoritative centrality of matrilineal autonomy and bonding (p. 22). Of the matrilineal "trinity," Eva, Hannah, and Sula Peace, the first is the "creator and sovereign" of the line (p. 23). She models strength and independence; Hannah spontaneity and sensuality. Sula subverts the old myths circulated by both white and black society about black women and then generates new ones in their stead. She is "the Amazon," a type of independent woman feared by other black women and deeply resented by the Black Lady, a socially appropriate type, which Nel has become. Sula's death, Nel's honestly confronting her memory, and Nel's accepting her own complicity in guilt finally allow her to reread her past with Sula and to rewrite it as a "text of Black/female friendship and bonding, or of matrilineal links between women in general" (pp. 24-25).

Like Maxine Hong Kingston's mythical woman warrior, Hua Mu-lan, today's woman warrior in reality is attacking the falsities of the historical past in order to allow women generally to create their own new texts, and so to shape their destiny.

105.   Prescott, Peter S. "Dangerous Witness."*Newsweek* (January 7, 1974): 63.

Sula is "an exemplary fable" (p. 63) of moral and spiritual entropy. It works on a richly symbolical level as it treats the mythic mysteries of sex, birth and death, fire and water, and yet it is also marked by simple, concrete set-pieces (on the town of Medallion and its characters) which create the novel's effect cumulatively on the very literal level.

*   Pullin, Faith. "Landscapes of Reality." *Black Fiction: New Studies in the Afro-American Novel Since 1945.* Cited above as item 75.

106.   Royster, Philip M. "A Priest and a Witch Against the Spiders and The Snakes: Scapegoating in Toni Morrison's *Sula*." *UMoja* n.s. 2 (1978): 149-68.

For the black people of the Bottom, Shadrack and Sula meet two critically important psychological needs. As scapegoat victims, both are blamed for the misery of the whole group, and as rescuers they are exemplary of how to escape the misery of the group.

Even as a soldier in WWI, Shadrack was a scapegoat victim. He returns shellshocked and withdrawn, and in the remainder of his life exacts revenge on society by becoming a kind of insane priest ritualistically attempting to save his people from death every year on January 3rd, National Suicide Day, a ceremonial occasion he instituted. That he in fact leads many of them to their deaths in the tunnel (a symbol of their persecution by majority society) at the very time when his own faith in the suicide ritual is diminished is one of the novel's bleak ironies.

Shadrack and Sula share the existential problem of loneliness. For her that is not metamorphosed into serene aloneness (peace) until her death. Like her counterpart, Sula is a willing victim for her best friend, Nel, the "representative of the townspeople's world view" (p. 153). Nel's feelings of guilt as persecutor and Sula's feelings of grief as victim are dramatized by their respective reactions to the funeral of Chicken Little, whom together they inadvertently drowned.

There is in the role of persecutor a degree of sadism which is brought out in Nel's relationship to her husband, Jude. Furthermore, a picture of modern existential independence can be found in Sula's stridently opposing her lifestyle to that of Nel and the community which, like a spider, weaves its web around and encloses her as its scapegoat victim. Another image, that of being like a snake, is used ostensibly for Sula (because of her birthmark), but is most accurately applied to the townspeople of the Bottom who consider Shadrack and her evil (devils) and consequently drive them out psychologically and persecute them with ostracism and gossip.

Believing herself the only vital, whole, colored woman she knows, Sula may in fact be an example of absolute loneliness even though she generates comfortable, supportive fantasies to delude herself at her life's end. She disturbs Nel's pat definition of what it means to be "good" (conformity to social norms); instead of living according to the community's prescription, Sula "produces good" in the lives of the Bottom's folk by motivating them to love and care for each other in reaction against the evil they assume they recognize in her.

Pariah that she is, Sula's passing away marks for the Bottom the "casting out of ...evil in their midst" (p. 165) and affords them a collective sigh of relief. Readers see they are transformed, alright, but for the worse. The scapegoat had contributed to their living better lives, even though they never realized it.

107. "Same Old Story." *TLS* 4 October, 1974, p. 1062.

The book concerns an entire black community that has survived unchanged in northern Ohio, its inhabitants ground down by self-mutilation, poverty, and grimness. Sula offends the natural pieties of the community through the exercise of her destructively pessimistic nature. She has fed her own courage and imaginativeness on the community, but refuses absolutely to be contained by it.

The story of the village known as the Bottom is clearly realized, but Sula's own story is not. She remains a character who exists only on the level of allegory, and as a result her death appears contrived to resolve the thematic complications she represents.

108. Shannon, Anna. "'We Was Girls Together': A Study of Toni Morrison's *Sula*." *MMis* 10 (1982): 9-22.

TM's fiction is "separatist" (as contrasted with that of other black authors who argue for assimilation) and involves central characters in "experimental journies" that challenge their own communities and the values of the American Dream (p. 9). For this author the primary value is "maintaining identity in the face of racism," (p. 10) a task which implicitly demands characters define themselves in intensely personal terms before exploring social responsibility.

Self-discovery, the struggle for personal freedom, occurs in *Sula* as a result of a comprehensive, sustained attack on patriarchal (i.e., conventional) values. The conventional view of romantic love is implicitly a constraint upon women's relationships to men, but more significantly upon women's friendships with each other and on their need to grow and seek self-fulfillment. For years the extremely close relationship between Nel and Sula strengthened them as individuals and provided each a buffer against the force of the outside world aimed to exact social conformity. TM's most serious indictment of conventionality is located in Nel's marriage, satisfying though that is to her, which isolates her from Sula and makes her one of "them," the women who have "folded themselves into starched coffins" (p.14). Nel blames Sula for the affair the latter has with her husband Jude. Conveniently she ignores the fact of her sexual possessiveness and allows the routines of marriage and respectability to spin "a steady gray web around her heart" (p. 15) that lodges there darkening her inner life for years.

Sula's directionless, destructive version of sexual equality, which she chooses to describe as acting like a man, is a threat to the community of the Bottom. She is emotionally isolated from everyone, even her mother whom she watches burn to death and her grandmother whom she has institutionalized. As death closes over her at 30, Sula clings stubbornly to the conviction that at least her fall has been her own, thus singular.

Male characters too, notably Shadrack and the deweys, but also Ajax and Jude, become victims of types of fatal conformity, and no one in the Bottom is aware until it is too late that without Sula as a living critique of their lives, white values will overwhelm them and their already tenuous sense of community will disappear.

Even Nel is slow to realize the vital importance of Sula, although the estranged women are tentatively reconciled just before Sula's death. Twenty-five years of reflection are necessary before Nel, middle aged and enriched by nothing but memory, can acknowledge her personal loss and through her particular grief suggest the more universal loss represented in the rupture of a soulmate relationship between two women. That bond was absolutely primary. To betray such a generative attachment because of sexist or racist social conventions is to betray oneself.

109. Smith, Barbara. "Beautiful, Needed, Mysterious." *Freedomways* 14 (1974): 69-72.

The reviewer's personal experience with the death of a grandmother convinces her TM's insights into life and death matters are comforting because they are true. The language she uses is marked by densely packed "mascon images" ("massive concentration of Black experiental energy which ...affects...Black speech, Black song, Black poetry," p. 70) as well as being rooted in the unique heritage of Afro-American life. The second most important formative influence on this author is gender. Like *TBE, Sula* is an "undeniably feminine" work (p. 70), this time about the relationship between two black girls whose lives "mesh immediately" from the time they first meet until they are grown up.

Their intimacy is finally shattered by Sula's casually sleeping with her friend Nel's husband. Sula's behavior is called "classically evil" by TM, but the reviewer accounts for it in sociological (not archetypal) terms. She calls Sula a nonconformist in a conforming period of time, and adds that "racial and sexual circumstance" (p. 71) prevented Sula's expressing herself in other, less-destructive ways.

Her life, lived entirely in terms of free self-expression, is a damning critique of the lives of quiet desperation maintained for so long by residents of the Bottom. Sula purges the community with her death, and yet her violation of the friendship she shares with Nel is a greater betrayal even than the fact that Nel's husband consequently deserts her.

The links between black women, so important in the novel, forged in youthful innocence and maintained without examination until after Sula's death, are renewed by Nel's realization years later that Sula was the most important person in her life.

110. Smith, Barbara. "Toward a Feminist Criticism." *In The Memory and Spirit of Frances, Zora, and Lorraine: Essays and Interviews on Black Women and Writing.* Edited by Juliette Bowles. Washington, D.C.: Howard University, 1979, pp. 32-40.

Motivated by black feminist and lesbian convictions, Smith argues that current women's studies are in a kind of "second wave," having begun with black feminists like Frances Harper in the 19th century. Smith's own function as critic is explicitly political and propagandistic, designed to attack the false assumption in the black community that sexual oppression (especially for black women) either does not exist or is "lightweight" compared to racial oppression. The undeniable reality is the "misogyny of black men, the hatred of women, and the consequent violence against them....The Richard Wrights, Leroi Joneses, Ed Bullinses and Ishmael Reeds who destroy black women in their works are legion...they...are threatening the very fabric of black life" (p. 34).

The point being driven home is that black women's writing and particularly black lesbian writing exists and demands to be recognized. That recognition has been slow in coming, even though the black feminist movement has evolved right along with a more general North American feminism.

Literary theory adequate to deal with black feminist literature must necessarily embody the realization that the politics of sex are as crucial as those of race and class (p.36). Secondly, that theory would tacitly assume "that black women writers constitute an identifiable literary tradition" (p.36). As a method, the primary evidence for the criticism of black feminist literature would be other works by black women--not a body of critical apparatus (p.37). In style, black feminist criticism would...be highly innovative" (p. 37), asserting the lesbian nature of works "not because women /in them/ are 'lovers,' but because they are...central,...positively portrayed, and have pivotal relationships with each other" (p. 37).

To illustrate, *Sula* is an "exceedingly lesbian novel" because its subject is a passionate friendship between women and its tone is implicitly critical of male/female relationships and of marriage and family. Women bond with each other because they are neither white nor male, and Sula herself is a strident illustration of the lesbian disavowal of patriarchial values. The kind of "secret" level of meaning in black feminist literature is a consequence of the nearly total suppression of identity that all black women (lesbian or not) have had to face. Without class or race privileges, sexual privilege is the only one black women enjoy.

111. Smith, Cynthia J. "Black Fiction By Black Females: *Sula.*" *Crosscurrents* 26 (Fall, 1976): 340-43.

Black females figure only incidentally in fiction by blacks generally or in novels by the two best known black authors of the 20th century: Richard Wright and Ralph Ellison. Singular exceptions to this rule can be found in work by Nella Larsen and Jessie Redmond Fausett during the Harlem Renaissance. But in the 1970's, fictional portraits of black women appeared in startling numbers and variety, forcing changes in old models by "transcending" those simple images and drawing complex, realistic black females.

In *Sula* TM creates a very special sense of place (Medallion, Ohio) and into it sets decidedly unconventional characters to work. Shadrack tries to order his personally shattering experience of WWII by instituting a National Suicide Day, a scheduled time devoted to death so that folks could manage by anticipation, by planning, the fearful unexpectedness of death and dying. Eva Peace conforms to none of the stereotypes of black (mammy) mothers. A woman deserted, left with the obligations of a single parent, Eva sacrifices her leg under the wheels of a train for insurance money to support her desperately needy family, but she also burns to death her junkie son, Plum, and--to complicate the portrait further--on another occasion she jumps from a second story window in a vain attempt to save her daughter Hannah from burning to death.

Sula, the central figure of the book, grows up believing she has no familial or social or communal obligations whatsoever. She takes

anything she wants from life--including other women's husbands--
because her natural creativity, her inclination to artistry and self-
expression, has no other outlet. In that, "Sula... is a symbol of the
black community whose lives are damned up and unexpressed" (p.
341).

112.   Spacks, Patricia Meyer. "Fiction Chronicle." *HudR* 27 (1974-75):
284.
 Sula is considered one of a group of new psychological novels
by women (with *Fear of Flying, Advancing Paul Newman,* and *Wait
Until Evening*) on the subject of female liberation and sexuality. But
TM's book is distinctive in that Sula is determinedly her own person
making her own life. The work has a kind of disjointed quality: it
emphasizes the bizarre in life (Chicken Little's drowning; Eva Peace
burning her son to death), it plays crucial events offstage, it blurs the
passage of great chunks of time, and it diminishes the effect of
narrative incident. All that appears to matter is what makes the self.
Unfortunately the reader cannot be certain what Sula has made of her
self. Her death is arbitrary, and the concluding section of the book is
hollow.

113.   Stein, Karen. " 'I Didn't Even Know His Name': Naming in Toni
Morrison's *Sula." Names* 28 (September, 1980): 226-29.
 Because naming has power and is a source of control, the fact
that Sula did not know her lover's (Ajax') true name underscores the
novel's ironic theme: how "uncertainties of human motivation and
mysteries of human identity impeded understanding, thus leading to
loss and betrayal" (p. 226).
 Characters' names function ironically or even satirically.
Women are named stereotypically, either for virtuous female models
or for their polar opposite: flagrant temptresses. But then the women
characters themselves illustrate the limitations inherent in such
conventional thinking. One family of women--the aptly-titled
Wrights--carry on "proper," scaled down, contracted, sanitary lives.
The other black matriarchy in the novel--the ironically named Peaces--
exist in a chaotic, extended family that is well acquainted with sex but
knows little of love. The single name Eva (clearly no Hebrew mother
figure) given to the three Deweys obliterates their identities and stunts
their growth. Eva's daughter, Hannah-- unlike the pious but barren
Biblical character for whom she is named--is a pagan earth-goddess.
 Sula's name is unique, and so it makes her unique. Like all
heroes, she needs no surname and accepts no limits on her behavior.
The names of all the other women characters in the book indicate their
descent from larger figures; Sula is herself bigger than life.
 Male names are similarly ironic. Ajax runs away from a
woman's love; Jude betrays his wife. Eva's husband is not Adam nor

even a man; he is merely BoyBoy. Shadrack has survived his own peculiar fiery furnace, but not through faith. He exists as a shell of a man, and is in constant dread of death.

Tragically, relationships founder because characters are unable to truly "know the names" of others. Too late Nel realizes the primacy of Sula in her life and cries out her name at Sula's burial. Characters remain locked within the prison of self, though, and their utter aloneness, their lack of comprehension, is symbolized by Sula's "I didn't even know his name."

114. Stein, Karen. "Toni Morrison's *Sula*: A Black Woman's Epic." *BALF* 18 (1984): 146-50.

The essay acknowledges TM's frequent use of mythic narrative structures, but asserts that it is really her ironic juxtaposing of mythic expectation with mundane reality that is most typical.

As double outsider (black, woman) in a white patriarchal society, TM the author must use ironic reversal of expectation to create a new definition of heroism. Her heroes must face the trials arising from powerlessness, from limitation, from loss, and from suffering. Nel and Sula represent the range of choices for black women in America: rigid conformity to convention, or total denial of orthodox communal values. The former tends to produce stagnation and passivity, the latter sensual freedom without direction (p.147). Neither affords personal fulfillment or social regeneration.

Sula is destroyed by her involvement in Chicken Little's death and becomes truly isolated, a pariah. Nel's marriage to Jude Greene also produces a "death" of her self.

Sula's quest for knowledge (college, travel, sexual liasons) brings about mere cynicism, not a hero's sense of power, and motivated by sheer empty restlessness, she seduces her best friend's husband and shatters their relationship. Instead of a transforming vision, Sula sees only her own sadness and alienation, and in the outrageousness of her deathbed vision of the last days (*Sula*, p. 125) the impossibly large gulf between ideal epic regeneration and the actuality of the fallen world of modern America is highlighted. Even her being a boon to her society is shown in negative terms: she gives them a focus for their animosity!

In Nel there is finally a movement toward enlarged self-awareness. Through her darker "second self," Sula, Nel realizes what a mixed capacity for good and evil is in people. Yet she does not so much triumph in the end as resign herself to accepting her fate and going ahead with the business of daily survival.

115. "Sula." *Booklist* 70 (March, 1974): 774.

The deep friendship between Nel and Sula is intense and eventually destructive. The two soulmates are themselves estranged by Sula's casually seducing Nel's husband, and the community at large is charged with hostility toward the immoral Sula, who sickens and dies essentially alone even though she has returned to the Bottom after a 10 year absence. Years later Nel comprehends Sula's true worth.

116. "Sula." KR 41 (November 1, 1973): 1225.

The conviction that she is "a major and formidable talent" (p. 1225) is reinforced by TM's impressive second novel, *Sula*. The metaphorically paired, singular characters, Shadrach and Sula, stand outside the community dependencies that bind other folks in the Bottom. Shadrach defies death by welcoming it once each year. Sula violates all notions of responsibility to family and/or friends, preferring to "stand against the sky" and finally to fall "like a redwood" (p. 1225) instead of rotting away like a stump.

117. "Sula." *Playboy* 21 (March, 1974): 22.

No slyly indirect work, this book affects readers deeply, like an ice pick wound. Two black women who share a profoundly disturbing secret are driven apart by the sexual indiscretion of one, yet they reconcile before death. The novel is "mournful" and "angry" and presented in language that is "pure and resonant" (p. 22).

118. "Sula." *PubW* 5 November, 1973, p. 56.

Sula begins life as a "different" kind of young black girl, and grows to become a pariah to her community. So evil do they consider her, they feel delivered when she dies. Then they discover they needed her more than they hated her.

119 "Sula." *VV* 7 March, 1974, p. 21.

In a black community beautifully created in prose, Sula lives a dangerously experimental life. Curiosity, not economics, as is characteristic of most novels about racial conflict, drives her to explore. But her discoveries--in sex, in family, and in friendship, the thematic centers of the book--are bitterly disappointing. Sula considers herself a solitary, independent figure. The town views her as a type of legendary evil. In the end, the novel's implicit allegory overwhelms it, and the characters' "reality /is/ subjugated to their meaning" (p 21).

"Morrison shows little sympathy for her characters and no revulsion either" (p. 21), so the reader remains very detached despite the implicitly tragic events being worked out in the fiction.

120. Thwaite, Anthony. "Borders of Fantasy." *The Observer* 23 November, 1980, p. 28.

  Sula is a more delicate novel than *SOS* and less weighed down by "Faulknerisms," yet its prose is flawed by strained attempts to be imagistic which are simply annoying ("the sun was already rising like a white hot bitch"). Sula and Nel grow up together, learn early that they are "neither white nor male, and that all freedom and triumph was forbidden to them" (p.28). Their paths part, Nel marrying and living conventionally, Sula leaving to lead a stubbornly iconoclastic existence. The book succeeds in showing "the power of superstition and the way love can become law" (p.28), but what TM's admirers call an inclination to write poetically ("He expected his story to dovetail into milkwarm commiseration") is in fact only bad mixed metaphor.

121. Uglow, Jennifer. "The folk at the Bottom." *TLS* 19   (December, 1980): 1442.

  TM's highly individualistic work, together with that of Nella Larsen (*Passing; Quicksand*), is, regrettably, the only fiction by a black American woman to have been published in England. In *TBE* and *Sula*, TM turned her cooly ironic view on "the process of growing up black, female and poor" (p.1442). Those books nostalgically evoke the lives of the black neighborhoods, but the warmth with which TM recalls life in an earlier time is consistently undercut by harsh reality. The only affection expressed to Pecola Breedlove comes from her father just before he rapes her. Similarly, in *Sula*, the same mother who puts her leg beneath a train for insurance money for her children will later hug her drug-addicted son one last time and then torch him to release him from what she judges to be his misery.

  There is laughter in *Sula*--at the reason for the name of the Bottom, at Shadrack's wacky intelligence in instituting National Suicide Day--but it is the kind of laughter that acknowledges a grim, bad joke. Sula herself becomes a disruptive power in the Bottom as she offends everyone--including her best friend, Nel--with her boundless sexual curiosity. Ironically Sula's presence binds the community together in mutual fear of and hostility toward her. Perhaps appropriately, she loses her lover only when she becomes like other women in the Bottom and decides to keep him in a "normal" and possessive way.

  All three of TM's novels look with disturbing ambivalence at both the past and the force of traditions (familial, racial), which the author implies must certainly be cherished. Nevertheless the honored past must be passed on without the humiliation that has been inherent in it. Thus her work both "explain/s/ the power of and give/s/ the lie to the cult of 'black is beautiful' " (p. 1442).

  TM makes more demands on the sensibilities of readers than do black male writers. Catastrophe, when it occurs in her writing, is not a result of failing to get ahead in the world at large, but instead is set within the intimacy of neighborhoods and families. Readers are robbed of stock responses and thus are more deeply unsettled by the fiction. Particularly painful is the conflict between generally capable, durable black women and the underdeveloped men they cherish. Her novels are technically sophisticated (complicated narratives, shifting perspectives) and, in their depiction of racial disenfranchisement, intensely political. Yet she offers no obvious solutions. The "worst illusion of all is hope" (p.1442) for her, and our best asset as we confront the grimness of real life can be our "humour, generosity, or passion" (p. 1442).

122.   Walters, Ray. "Paperbacks: New and Noteworthy: *Sula* and *Tar Baby*" *NYTBR* 4 April, 1982, p. 35.
         With the publication of TM's second and fourth novels in paperback editions, readers can "observe the artistic development of a leading American black woman novelist" (p. 35). In the earlier work, she created a "somewhat icy myth," and in the latter she gets beyond social realism to shape a "symbolic fable of race and eroticism" (p. 35).

123.   Yardley, Jonathan. "The Naughty Lady." *BIW* (February 3, 1974): 3.
         The real achievement of *Sula* is its resonant prose which can shape such sharply realized figures as Sula and Eva Peace and a sense of place fully as evocative as that of Flannery O'Connor or Eudora Welty--even though TM should not be considered a southern writer.

PART V
CRITICISM OF SPECIFIC WORKS: *SONG OF SOLOMON*

March 30, 1981 / $1.25

Newsweek

Black Magic

Novelist Toni Morrison

124.   Atlas, Marilyn Judith. "A Woman Both Shiny and Brown: Feminine Strength in Toni Morrison's *Song of Solomon*." *SSMLN* 9 (1979): 8-12.

The novel explores the relation between material ownership of things and spiritual freedom. The central figure, Pilate, is through her mythic power able to make her solution to the thematic dilemma--surrender to the air, to spirituality--"not only a possible /resolution/ but /also/ the only viable one" (p. 8).

Milkman is caught and must choose between the materialistic, power-oriented values of his father, and the transcendent, spiritual values of his Aunt Pilate. Her presence in the action of the first scene, singing the Song of Solomon, comforting Ruth Foster Dead, tips the scale toward spirituality and provides the first prenatal influence on Milkman. At the age of six he will be disillusioned to discover that man cannot fly, but upon reaching the sixth grade he is drawn to Pilate's home again (as she attracts his unwilling father to her house filled with music and joy), and this time Milkman's discovery is very affirmative: he intuits he will never let this fascinating, strong-willed, feminine role model go.

By following the information she provides, Milkman finds the roots of his family and his name. He learns to discard that which keeps him earthbound, and to be "indifferent to his earthly fate" (p. 11). The spirituality which Pilate represents and which Milkman embraces passionately is traditionally female, nurturing, forgiving. "Hers is the power of traditional western goddesses" (p. 12), combining spiritual wisdom with natural fecundity, the combination subsequently overpowering "traditional male values of ownership and judgement" (p. 13).

125.   Atlas, Marilyn Judith. "The Darker Side of Toni Morrison's *Song of Solomon*." *SSMLN* 10 (1980): 1-13.

Major figures in *SOS* do nothing actively to change the society that discriminates against them. They accept the distortions of their world and if they strike out at all, do so merely against each other. Only minor characters, Guitar Bains and other members of the radically violent group The Seven Days, direct their anger at the white power structure. TM makes these minor characters sympathetic so the reader is forced to consider them seriously and to decide for him/herself about the legitimacy of political violence.

Guitar maintains that violence can be rational, although Milkman disagrees and says Guitar will have his individual humanity destroyed by his commitment to an eye-for-an-eye killing. Evidence of the destructive effect of violence appears in the case of Robert Smith, the distraught insurance agent, who tries vainly to fly in the novel's opening scene, as well as in the instance of the pathetic Henry Porter, who finally learns to love instead of merely hating. His newly learned ethic leads to a vital relationship with Macon Dead's daughter Corinthians.

All of the members of The Days are deeply frustrated, "desperate for change and for some control over their lives" (p. 5). Yet only Guitar maintains his enthusiasm for spiritual transcendence so that in the end the reader sees he too, like Milkman, is capable of flight. Guitar is made by the author to be a physically attractive, brave, sensitive character, one who defends his friend in a fight with school mates and later becomes the liberating force in Milkman's life. But his character is also made darkly ambiguous. Early in his life, Guitar encounters shocking injustice in the death of his father and is deeply embittered by that. He is estranged from other blacks, especially those who are not as outraged as he at white society or those who themselves live luxuriously amid social injustice. In his politicized pursuit of what he terms rational justice, he begins to despise and distrust all people, even his erstwhile best friend. That he needs the violent dogma of The Days to justify his own existence is shown by his decision that Milkman too must die, if for no other reason than the fact that he is "guilty" of having too little social conscience. Psychologically speaking, Guitar must kill his "brother" (the other) in order to eradicate that part of himself that will not focus exclusively on racial justice.

The author steadfastly refuses to judge Guitar, however. For her, "good and evil evade definition" (p. 12). That he is "distorted" as a character does not make him evil. In fact he has as much possibility of spiritual transcendence as Milkman. Should each surrender to the air, each may ride it. What TM does is make each reader responsible for sorting out the moral ambiguity of Guitar and The Days.

*   Bakerman, Jane. "Failures of Love: Female Initiation in the Novels of Toni Morrison." *AL*. Cited above as item 59.

126.   Barksdale, Richard K. "Song of Solomon." *WLT* 52 (Summer, 1978): 465.

TM's literary achievement with *SOS* is as revolutionary as was the work of Karl Marx in political thought. Her novel turns upside down many longstanding value assumptions of western European culture. Even the title of her book plays ironically against the Biblical suggestion of a love song. In TM's hands the title is used to refer to an Afro-American slave song and to the heroic Solomon's flight back to his homeland. Similarly, names such as Pilate, Circe, and Mary Magdelena--loaded as they are with historical connotations--are inverted and used in ways which are "empty of traditional symbolic import" (p. 465).

Perhaps most importantly, Aristotelian conventions regarding narrative structure (beginning, middle, end) are violated. "The pattern of narration is circular, not linear" (p.465) and is characterized by frequent, apparently random digressions. The probable, the possible, and the actual are not at all clearly distinguished, nor are past and present tense kept separable in a traditional way. Yet the result is not to render the work unintelligible, but rather to give to the slave history of blacks in America a unique kind of cogency. The fact that the work coheres despite apparent discontinuities is a tribute to TM's artistry.

127   Barthold, Bonnie J. "Toni Morrison, *Song of Solomon.*" *Black Time, Fiction of Africa, The Caribbean, and The United States.* New Haven and London: Yale University Press, 1981, pp. 174-84.

Africans experience time as a cyclic, mythic progression, not in the linear, historical manner of westerners. In the former scheme, time includes and belongs to the community as a whole; cyclic recurrence (of seasons, birth/death, spirit appearances) is the normal order of things.

A major consequence of being enslaved by western cultures was the attempt to rob black people of their sense of time. Slaveholders believed they "owned" the time of those people they purchased, and thus blacks generally were cut off from their past and denied the freedom to determine their destiny in the present or future. Yet African resistance to cultural and temporal dispossession has remained tenaciously effective, as evidenced even now by the striking capacity of African culture to maintain native institutions even while absorbing foreign influences into itself. This resiliance is apparent in the historical resistance to the fact of slavery, in the blending of African and Christian religious concepts and practices, as well as in the merging of African and western elements in modern language and music. So it is that in black fiction the confrontation between Africa and Europe (i.e., between myth and history), between certainty and flux, is dramatically revealed through the role and function of time.

Milkman Dead, protagonist of *SOS,* is caught between two conflicting views of time, a fragmented one represented by his father and a unified one by his Aunt Pilate. The novel works toward a resolution that fuses the past (African) and the present into a "song" of heritage.

Music structures the opening scene of the novel by establishing the relationship between the song of Sugarman, the song of Solomon, and the belief held by some Africans that one's spirit flies back to the home of the ancestors after death. This relationship becomes evident to readers only with hindsight, however. That triumphal flight by the ancestral Solomon, commemorated in song by adults and children alike, denotes spiritual triumph and the "redemption of time into a sacred continuum" (p. 176). Similarly, the incapacity for flight (Robert Adams in scene one, the peacocks seen by Milkman and

Guitar midway through the novel) signals spiritual oppression. Thus TM's fiction technique requires the reader to look for unity among apparently fragmented narrative bits and to perceive in that implicit unity the invisible, mythic continuum of time and identity.

Representing opposing functions of time are Milkman's father, Macon, and his Aunt, Pilate. The former has repudiated the past, present, and future, and thus dispossessed himself, he seeks satisfaction in temporal dispossession of others by virtue of owning things. Pilate, to the contrary, plays a mythically conceived role: she carries her past and the previous history of others with her; she intermediates between the material and spiritual worlds; she is a "Keeper of Time." Caught between these representatives of disorder and order--the theme which carries TM's first two novels--and the object of the conflict between them is Milkman. Earlier TM's moves toward reconciliation between disorder and order were incomplete. In *TBE,* Pecola's baby, fathered by her father, dies and she slips into insanity. In *Sula,* Nel Greene is estranged from her soul mate Sula and only becomes aware of that and of her consequent spiritual loss after the mysterious, emblematic Sula's death.

In *SOS*, the conflict between chaos and order is symbolically resolved in Milkman. He and Pilate are heirs of a mythic heritage alluded to in the fact that their common ancestor Solomon could fly and in the otherwise unexplained fact that the first Macon Dead is said to have been born in two locations simultaneously (Macon, Georgia, and Shalimar, Virginia). The discovery by Milkman and Pilate of this heritage allows readers to understand the way in which *SOS* redeems and celebrates the fictional descendants of Macon as well as the historically dispossessed blacks who lived "below Macon" in what W.E.B. DuBois called "that strange land of shadows" (The Souls of Black Folks), and by so redeeming them reestablishes them in the black, mythic continuity of time.

128.   Blake, Susan. "Folklore and Community in *Song of Solomon.*" *MELUS* 7 (Fall, 1980): 77-82.

The source for and basis of *SOS* is a Gullah folktale concerning African-born slaves who one day fly back to Africa. With its emphasis on community, folklore like this clearly reveals TM's central theme of the relationship between individual and community.

Communal values implicit in the folktale of flight emphasize a common dream (ability to fly), a common disappointment (loss of that ability through bondage as slaves), and a group identity. Milkman's discovery of the truth of the "Song of Solomon" symbolizes his immersion (as an individual) in "more inclusive communities: his family, Afro-Americans, all blacks" (p. 78).

Community is in fact both the end and the means of Milkman's quest. He finds his links with his ancestors in developing connections with contemporaries, including his mother, sisters, Aunt Pilate,

Sweet, and men he hunts with in Virginia. The model of communal values inherent in folk consciousness and Milkman's mentor throughout his quest is Pilate. She is sharply contrasted with her brother Macon whose selfish individualism ostensibly represents "progress."

But the comfortable pattern of individuals finding identity within community is violated disturbingly by the novel's close. Milkman does not so much unite with Pilate as succeed her upon her death; his leap toward his killing friend Guitar suggests the embracing of individualistic risk more than a relationship. The sense of identity achieved at the end of the work is more nearly individualistic than communal, and thus it forces readers to face disquieting realities looming ahead for the black community.

In nearly all their prototypical forms, the stories of flying Africans concern groups, crowds, boatloads, i.e., communities. Yet in the novel, Solomon wings away alone, abandoning numerous children and a grieving wife. Morrison alters the folktale's emphasis in order to shift the stress away from the traditional black definition of community as group unified by national origin or political condition. Instead what preoccupies TM is the fact of conflict between personal and political communities and the consequent need to opt for a definition on the personal level. The conflict between personal and political communities is what separates Milkman and Guitar, because the latter, out of a sense of political community has set out to kill his brother, a member of a personal community. Milkman learns what Guitar forgets--the bottom-line value of "kinship...brotherhood" (p. 81).

Thus "community" as TM defines it in the novel is a function of individual, caring, decent relationships, and it is a definition which emerges only after the action of the novel has turned explicitly away from the sense of "political" community that opened the work.

In TM's view, the basic situation for blacks has changed, and with it the definition of community. The communal sense that bound blacks to each other in opposition to whites is gone; now it seems that very racial concept of community threatens to violate a concept of personal community which would focus its attention on the interpersonal relations characteristic of contemporary reality.

129. "Books Briefly: *Song of Solomon.*" *Progressive* 42 (January, 1978): 50.

Even though surrounded by all the material comfort his middle class family can provide, Milkman Dead is in truth impoverished, because he lacks knowledge of his family's secret background. His Aunt Pilate leads him on a search for that knowledge, and the reader thus enters "a magic landscape" and there observes Milkman struggling to distinguish "family myth from historic truth" (p. 50).

130. Bowman, Diane Kim. "Flying High: The American Icarus in Morrison, Roth, and Updike." *PCL* 8 (1982): 10-17.

Informing the quests of TM's Milkman, Roth's Portnoy and Updike's Rabbit is the myth of Icarus, "the would-be solar hero" (p. 10), a phallic, ego-centered character whose trials gratify only self. Flight is the metaphor used to articulate the myth, but although it is flight from authority and repression toward freedom, by its very nature that flight ends in failure that is the equivalent of a fall.

The American Icarus is an underachieving male nagged by self-doubt into constant sexual fantasies or activities. When foiled, as he must be because flight upward is finite and sexual engagement produces detumescence, the Icarian figure "falls back" into dependency and boredom, frequently associated with feelings of dread for women.

Of the three protagonists, only Milkman appears to escape the implicit defeat symbolized by the myth. Milkman is a very dependent, selfish character who exercises himself casually on women-- especially Hagar. Twice he flies literally, once by plane, the last time when he leaps toward his brother-enemy Guitar. He seems to grow personally, in knowledge of his roots and discovery of his potential, but the image of flight at the end of the book remains stubbornly ambiguous. Whether his launching himself from Solomon's Leap is as clearly suicidal as Robert Smith's idiotic plunge from (No) Mercy Hospital, or as selfish as Solomon's abandonment of wife and children, it clearly cannot include either "literal flight or the safe landing to a controlled leap. Milkman...plunges, in darkness, to the earth" (p. 13).

Because he alone of the three main figures "experiences a kind of journey to the underworld" (p. 16), and thus through death, Milkman does not remain trapped in adolescence, typically the fate of the Icarian character. Portnoy attempts to escape from his mother and toward personal freedom, and his "flight" is conceived consistently in terms of "sex--free sex, sex with no commitments" (p.13). From gratification to renewed urge--Portnoy is trapped forever in a cyclic, fruitless quest. Rabbit's flight (and Jerry's in *Marry Me*) is away from the world of "commitments to work or to people" (p. 14) and toward total self-gratification.

A number of these figures in American literature attempt to gain their freedom and achieve the kind of masculinity that bestows hero status, but failing to get free of the mother, having as a goal phallic self-satisfication, their soaring flights lead merely to precipitous falls.

131. Bruck, Peter. "Returning To One's Roots: The Motif of Flying in Toni Morrison's *Song of Solomon*." *The Afro-American Novel Since 1960*. Edited by Peter Bruck and Wolfgang Karrer. Amsterdam: Gruner Publishing, 1982, pp. 289-305.

Contrary to early black female writers who stressed the dilemma of being trapped by circumstances, contemporary authors are focusing on self-affirmation. In *SOS*, the concern TM showed for folklore in her first books is wedded to a quest for family roots--ultimately to be found in the Afro-American cultural heritage.

The narrative spans 50 years of family history, and is presented through a series of multiple, omniscient points of view, so that the author's presence is felt together with various personalized narrators.

Milkman's father is a type of "living dead" because he is totally cut off from his heritage and has given himself up to acquiring material wealth. Milkman eventually separates himself from the property-centered world of his parents and begins his odyssey. Herein *SOS* uses elements of the novel of initiation: departure from the known and familiar world and confrontation with the unknown and strange leading to insight. Notably missing from the pattern is the figure of a Tempter. Afro-American fiction does not use the scene of disillusionment, but substitutes for that cynical awareness the more positive recognition of one's ancestry (pp. 294-295).

In the all-black community of Shalimar during a night-long coon hunt, Milkman comes to that recognition. He also learns the legend of his grandfather Jake and great-grandfather Solomon who had acquired the mythic ability of flight. The metaphor of flight as symbol of social exclusion has preoccupied black writers since the 1940's when blacks were excluded from flying in combat. It has also functioned as a collective wish fulfillment, either in the sense of escaping past or present conditions, or in the sense of returning to one's roots. Folk tales abound from slave times, organized around the fact of flying home to Africa or the Caribbean.

Thus Pilate is reconciled to her roots, dies, and flies off. Similarly Milkman uncovers his heritage, symbolically embraces his alter ego Guitar, and also takes flight.

Flight-signifying-mobility (geographic and sexual) appears to be a metaphor most appropriate to male figures. When women attempt to use it, they separate themselves from the community in very negative ways. Counterbalancing the metaphor of flight for men is that of singing for women (p. 303). Against the rather pessimistic depiction of black womanhood is set the ideal notion of a man and a woman coming together in an affirmtive, sensual way that is derived from the loving union modeled in the biblical Song of Solomon I: 15-16.

32.   Burke, Virginia M. "Song of Solomon." *LibJ* 102 (September 1, 1977): 1782-83.

Milkman Dead has women and prestige and a soft job afforded by his slumlord father's money, but he has never been enriched in significant, non-material ways--for instance by knowing either love or vitality--except once when he was 12, on the occasion of his visit to his Aunt Pilate's wine house. At 32, still living an aimless, dissolute

114

life, he sets out on a quest for gold, but the odyssey leads instead to
hard-earned self-knowledge.

SOS deftly combines the folk tradition of Hurston with the
Gothic tradition of Demby and Ellison as TM dramatizes the values
clashes that separate people from their own humanity.

133. Butler, Robert James. "Open Movement and Selfhood in Toni
Morrison's *Song of Solomon*." *CentR* 28-29 (Fall-Winter, 1984-85):
58-75.

The journey motif is central to both American and Afro-
American literary traditions. It is a means to dramatize the concept of
a quest, and, more explicitly, a quest that values pure movement, the
"process of endless becoming rather than progress culminating in a
state of completed being" (p.59). Its emphasis on human liberation
(instead of on reaching a place) distinguishes American and Afro-
American literary uses of movement from that observable in *The
Odyssey* or *Tom Jones* or *Robinson Crusoe*. Additionally that
emphasis on becoming renders invalid the sort of recent critical
assumption which suggests black fiction is either flatly static or a
"cyclical nightmare" (p. 60).

Black narrative presents open movement very affirmatively, and
in TM's work such movement is set in opposition to the characters'
option of accepting fixed values of traditional community life. Thus
we see in *Sula* that Nel's settling for a definite role in the community
is played against Sula's aggressive, determined restlessness.
Moreover *TB* concludes with Jadine in open motion while Son seeks
his place in a traditional society.

That dialectic is at the center of *SOS*, yet no simplistic synthesis
affirming the myth of movement appears in the end to render the novel
naive. TM works determinedly toward openness. For instance, the
setting is established as both fixed (a town on Lake Superior in Upper
Michigan) and fluid (an unnamed place, unlocalized and indefinite
although detailed). Similarly characters are ambiguous. Milkman's
mother and sisters remain "landlocked" creatures and Dr. Foster and
Macon II are paralyzed, stagnant types, made numb by their
circumstances or uncertain sense of self. Yet Milkman and Pilate both
undergo liberating wanderings, each a process of self-discovery.
Pilate's whole life reflects values of the American picaresque tradition.
She wanders for years, all the while enlivening her humanity, and in
the end she achieves a mystical kind of self-awareness epitomized by
energy and by singing. Milkman too, after age 30, "lights out" and
escapes the ennervating dependency--familial, sexual, fraternal--that
threatens to keep him always an instance of arrested development.

However despite the novel's closing references to soaring and to
mythic flight, that ending cannot be read reductively. It is "tangled
with ironies, paradoxes, and contradictions" (p. 70) suggesting both
Milkman's limited consciousness and the ironic, superior awareness

of the narrator. Earlier the narrator had used an episode involving Hansel and Gretel to allow readers to grasp what the character does not: the journey will involve dangerous encounters, not simple escape (p. 71). The narrator is highly ambiguous about the Deep South: it does contain a usable past, but also a destructive, maiming history (p. 71). Milkman intends to benefit Pilate, but he brings about her death. His awareness of "soaring" is romantic, even heroic. The narrator's is far more realistic. Combined, the two perspectives absolutely prevent one assigning a definitive meaning to the ending. It could well be that Milkman's "flight" is ultimately equated with the demented act of Robert Smith plunging to his death in the opening (p.73). So we have in the final analysis a work that is "an open dialectic, a set of ideas in motion rather than a neatly resolved narrative" (p. 73).

If any figure comes close to realizing transcendence in an unequivocal way, it is Pilate, whose restless movement never keeps her from caring for those she loves. With Pilate, TM breaks new literary ground, showing that the liberating movement of picaresque fiction is indeed available to women (p. 75).

* Clark, Norris."Flying Black: Toni Morrison's *The Bluest Eye, Sula,* and *Song of Solomon." MV.* Cited above as item 62.

134. De Arman, Charles. "Milkman As The Archetypal Hero: 'Thursday's Child Has Far To Go.'" *Obsidian* 6 (Winter, 1980): 56-59.
After establishing, with a bit of a quibble on what constitutes the "middle" of the week, that Milkman's birthdate falls on that kind of turning point, the author claims his birth places him at a "point in time where the past (his heritage) intersects his future (his ultimate encounter with life" (p. 56).

Milkman's story follows the three part structure of a mythic hero (separation, initiation, return) and closely resembles the pattern of the archetypal quest figure. Especially noteworthy are the "rites of birth," including the father's attempt to take the child's life, the protection afforded him by Pilate (his quasi-mystical mentor and guide), and the perilous journey which includes a literal meeting with Circe and a journey through the cave/underworld. In Shalimar, Milkman undergoes a series of crucial trials, so that ultimately he "becomes master of the world of men and of the Gods" (p. 59) in his transfiguration into a symbolic figure.

135. De Weever, Jacqueline. "Toni Morrison's Use of Fairy Tale, Folk Tale, and Myth in *Song of Solomon." SFQ* 44 (1980): 131-44.

116

SOS is so informed by elements borrowed from traditional literature (names, narrative elements, themes) that it can be said to be TM's folk tale. But she does not use her borrowings in traditional ways. Her intent is ultimately ironic, thus the analysis here is focused on the inversions the novelist has made.

Typically, men's names have a folk quality to them (Guitar, Milkman) and define the character; women's names reinforce the various ironies of their situations (e.g., Pilate does not "wash her hands of" her family but serves them all she can). In Part II of the book, Circe is associated with the witch of "Hansel and Gretel" and also with the enchantress figure of Homer. Pilate is discussed as a type of good witch, a fairy tale creature with the power of enchantment through song (p. 136).

Elements of the traditional narrative of flight are borrowed from the story of Daedalus and Icarus, and those are combined with the fairy tale notion of transcending human limitation. Milkman's story is derived in part from "Rumpeltstilskin" and from "Jack and the Beanstalk." Milkman is a character whose name TM associates with the spinning of gold from straw story. There the happy ending turns on discovering the dwarf's secret name. So too Milkman's journey in the book is designed to teach him the real name of his ancestors. The beanstalk tale lies back of Milkman's efforts to develop an independent sense of himself separate from the dominance of his father (p. 139), as does an episode in the novel concerning a strutting white peacock on the roof of a building where Buicks are sold. Both bear psychologically on Milkman's need for self-knowledge.

In the subplot, the love story of Corinthians and Porter is the inverse of the Hans Christian Anderson tale, "The Swineherd," with the black princess Corinthians finally accepting the love of her social and economic inferior and being happy forever after as a result (pp. 140-141).

References to fairy tale evolve at last into family legend, as Milkman's erroniously conceived pursuit of gold "becomes the pursuit of the song which yields the nugget of /the family's/ identity" (p. 143) and his own personal identity.

The ending is not so explicit as to be a true fairy tale because one cannot tell whether Milkman really flies. Certainly the conclusion suggests, though, that his journey has led to substantial self-awareness.

136.   Duvall, E.S. "Song of Solomon." *Atl* 240 (October, 1977): 105.

Done in the Roots tradition, *SOS* adds to the body of work by American blacks dealing with how "their unique heritage shapes identity" (p. 105). This latest book by TM is a family history tracing the literal and symbolic odyssey of Milkman Dead as he searches for gold and finds instead elements of familial and personal truth culminating in his discovery of his true family name.

The novel's language is derived from a folklore tradition, and TM's gallery of characters is varied and unforgettable.

137. Ellman, Mary. "Seven Recent Novels." *YR* 47 (June, 1978): 592ff.
    SOS holds up before us not the author's personal egotism, but the "egotism of group, the American blacks" (p.597). In Milkman and Lena and Corinthians, one is made sharply aware of the pathos of wasted human lives, and in Guitar of the frightening randomness of violence. Other characters, such as Pilate and Porter, "blossom" and become more affirmative models. Dialogue is vivid, unforgettable.

138. Fredrick, Earl. "The Song of Milkman Dead." *Nat* 225 (November 19, 1977): 536.
    TM may use urban settings for her fiction, but its tone is never anarchistic like that of her black contemporaries. She presents tight communities of blacks who share a kind of intimacy because of their common oppression, and she looks nostalgically at the values of and bonding within such communities.
    Her characters in *SOS* reveal a deep, abiding need for love. TM focuses the theme by acquainting us with the wise, tough, almost mystically natural Aunt Pilate who aids the novel's protagonist in his quest for manhood. A kind of mythic success crowns Milkman's search, but that is not to say the book is one which effects male redemption through feminine saving graces. Most of the women are, in fact, weaker than the men. Milkman's sister, Corinthians, faces the harshly bleak predicament of being an aging spinster in search of a committed relationship even though she knows that racism has conspired to make the pool of black men with stable, lucrative work very small indeed. Ruth, Milkman's mother, is a "Jocasta type" whose needs are both unique to her situation and also universal.
    If there is a black author today who can demonstrate to readers generally that black fiction is crafted from universal, human content, it is Toni Morrison.

139. Gardner, John. "John Gardner on Fiction." *NRep* 177 (December 3, 1977): 34.
    That *SOS* may not be a realistic representation of black life in America in no way diminishes its being a first rate accomplishment. Characters are uniquely named and a delight to know. Moreover its narrative organization and its thematic structure are wonderfully made.

140. Garnick, Vivian. "Into the Dark Heart of Childhood." *VV* 29 August, 1977, p. 41.

Ultimately *SOS* is unsatisfactory, the book's structure so manipulative that characters have more of an existence dictated by the structure than a genuine life of their own. As a result, Milkman's mythic quest into "the heart of the fear of leaving childhood" (p. 41) is not credible. It may be that Morrison is doomed because she chose the perspective of a male character whose essential reality she cannot communicate as truly as that of her anguished, stifled female figures.

141. Govan, Sandra Y. "Song of Solomon." *Cresset* 41 (May, 1978): 26.

On one, relatively literal, level, TM's award winning new novel concerns a "Dead" family. Macon, the father, is descended from a freed slave mistakenly registered under the name of "Dead." In fact members of the family have grown emotionally inert to the point of death, and they are distanced from (i.e., dead to) their African heritage both by loss of their true name and by the historical fact of slavery.

On a metaphorical level, the novel treats the Dead family's learning to live. Milkman is nominally the main character, an unwitting student of cultural anthropology and history who comes to full understanding of the oral history of his family and its relation to Africans who possessed the magical ability to fly.

What all the Deads must face are the facts of living, coming to terms with their past, accepting each other's weaknesses in the present, enduring racial conflict, surviving day to day on the level of "the street," bearing up under the bleakness of loveless relationships-- and even pursuing ennobling dreams. The weaving together of "the mundane, the mythic, and the mystical" makes this a brilliant novel (p. 26).

142. Harris, A. Leslie. "Myth as Structure in Toni Morrison's *Song of Solomon*." MELUS 7 (Fall, 1980): 69-76.

In *SOS* Morrison has used myth not in the most traditional sense of "a reality lived," but as a symbolical art form: mythopoesis (p. 69). Afro-American, Judeo-Christian, and Greco-Roman myth all merge in the author's own reshaping of the archetype of the hero and his quest.

Milkman's career follows the pattern of mythic figures such as Achilles (birth, alienation, quest, confrontation, reintegration), in that he develops psychologically and physically into a knowing, committed hero. He discovers during his quest the song that mythologizes his own heritage, and even overcomes the last enemy-- denial and despair--represented in his murderous friend and nemesis, Guitar.

Narrative structure in the work is not linear, but rather an "interlace" of plot and subplots through "a present which spans three generations" (p. 71). Circumstances of Milkman's birth are symbolically mythical: subterfuge is involved in his conception and delivery; Pilate--the attendant at his birth--is a social outcast and member of a "humbler order;" and the child himself becomes a focus of the father's hostility against his wife. Also, Milkman's birth is explicitly associated with the metaphor of flight (Icarus motif), which, during the second stage of his growth he does, by thoughtlessly rejecting parental authority, family ties, and love.

Getting rid of all "the shit that weighs you down" means (for Guitar) abandoning relationships and investing his energy in vengeance against whites. For Milkman the white peacock is significant in a more positive way, pointing to a picaresque adventure that takes him deeper and deeper into his family's past. The dream core of his quest is guarded by Circe, a type of witch in the land of the dead, whose revelations about his father and grandfather lead Milkman to Virginia where by fighting and hunting he acquires a degree of natural prowess which affords him requisite self-esteem. His return to his own world is ambivalent, though, in part because he cannot reconcile his father with his Aunt Pilate, the "novel's clearest representative of personal and racial heritage and continuity with the past" (p. 75). What matters for Milkman's mythic heroism in the end is not whether he overcame Guitar, but the fact that he symbolically affirms his and his world's values. In leaping to fight his enemy (despair, nihilism, sterility) the hero has already won (p. 75). He has accepted his past in its historical and supernatural aspects and also accepted himself.

143. Howard, Maureen. "Song of Solomon." *HudR* 31, no.1 (Spring, 1978): 186.

Part of a reader's pleasure in experiencing *SOS* comes from its use of oral traditions such as telling how places (the Bottom, Not Doctor Street) and characters (Milkman, Pilate, Sing and Sweet) are named. Such material is at once both history and reality heightened into myth. TM combines the language of the Bible and that of street blacks and engagingly presents both the humor of genteel black pretentions as well as the moving pathos of a woman grieving at her dead daughter's funeral.

144. Jefferson, Margo. "Black Gold." *Newsweek* 12 September, 1977, p.93.

This author's narratives treat black, midwestern neighborhoods, within which individuals struggle to reconcile the demands of family and/or culture with their personal needs. Frequently the results are tragic. In *TBE* a young girl goes mad; in *Sula* a fiercely independent woman eventually finds herself facing her illness and death alone.

Now with her third book TM is winning national acclaim (Book of The Month Club Selection) but in fact the novel is "flashier and more accessible..." but also "...less striking and less original" than earlier work (p.95A). Born into a family deeply embittered toward one another, Milkman Dead follows rumors of a lost family fortune in gold, and finds instead the treasure of their past. The heritage of the Deads (and, by suggestion, other blacks) contains crushing oppression, but also "exhilarating...strengths and possibilities" (p.96). Structural embellishments (frequent subplots) and numerous peripheral (if interesting) characters "weaken the focus" of the book (p. 96). Those just discovering Morrison should read back in her other work.

145.   Johnson, Diane. "The Oppressor in The Next Room." *NYRB* 10 November, 1977, p. 6ff.
    Before analyzing *SOS* briefly as a "picaresque and allegorical saga" of the Dead family in search of their roots, the reviewer creates a context for clearer and deeper understanding of reader response to TM's fiction.
    A bitterly discouraging theme of victimization runs through TM's two earlier novels as well as being a principal concern of her newest book, *SOS*. What is so startling is that the victimization of blacks by whites is merely a context for the fictions; that is not its subject. Blacks victimizing other blacks is. Many readers, both black and white, avoid thinking about or discussing the discomfitting statements her novels actually make. Whites frequently are uncertain whether the works are "artistically but not literally true" (p. 6) and they may be ashamed to admit that accepting the harsh content of the novels at face value is a kind of extension of their own racism. On the other hand, since all people, regardless of color, are what they are for reasons generally not of their own making, the most serious and potentially troubling question becomes whether Morrison's fictional black people ought to be as they are?
    The question itself is awkward to raise, the answer painful to consider, because the fact is that characters in Morrison's work (and that of Gayl Jones) consistently brutalize each other. Oppressive racism abounds, there can be no gainsaying that. But the threat of rape or physical abuse or abandonment or being set afire comes most immediately from "the oppressor in the next room, or in the same bed, or no farther away than across the street" (p.6).
    Impressions given by TM and Jones are gloomy indeed, and they are forcing audiences to radically alter their understanding of "the black experience," an understanding that has heretofore been based on impressions given by black male (Ralph Ellison, Richard Wright) authors whose primary preoccupation in their fiction was how to make it in a white world. Little attention was given by the latter writers to the unique vulnerability of women and girls when they are turned on by defeated, hopeless men.
    Milkman Dead's quest for his origins makes the novel appear derivative of Roots. However it has Morrison's stamp of originality

in its cast of striking female figures, and horrific and mythic events again jam her narrative--as in *Sula*

The cumulative effect of the book is to unbalance the reader. Whether to take her material as merely symbolic (and not a shocking representation of actual conditions), or whether to see her vision of domestic violence as literally true and thus unimaginably terrible-- those are the reader's choices.

146.   Kaiser, Ernest. "Recent Books." *Freedomways* 17 (1977): 187.

SOS unfortunately concerns another group of bizarre, stereotyped TM characters whose lives supposedly chronicle the experience of four generations of blacks. Alex Haley's *Roots* is a bad novel, but its people are real. John O. Killens's *Youngblood* and Margaret Walker's *Jubilee* both treat real, healthy blacks over the course of time. TM's novels are not real; they are "fantasy, fable, myth, allegory, magic superstition" (p. 187). White critics who know nothing about blacks extol her fiction, but it "is not the black experience" (p. 187).

147.   Kuehl, Linda. "Song of Solomon." *SR* 4 (September 17, 1977): 41.

Her third book is still another in the series of TM's "revolutionary" works whose heroes are in "defiance against a historyless past" (p. 41). Sula's faith was invested purely in herself. Milkman Dead's killing leap at the conclusion of *SOS* is evidence of his faith in the future. That faith emerged from his regenerative discoveries about his personal past and that of his family. Morrison is doing no less than "forging the uncreated consciousness of her race" (p. 41)

*   Lange, Bonnie Shipman. "Toni Morrison's Rainbow Code." *Crit.* Cited above as item 69.

148.   Lardner, Susan. "Books, Word of Mouth." *NYorker* 53 (November 7, 1977): 217ff.

SOS represents TM at her storytelling best. Its narrative line is intricate, but like the oral traditions upon which it is built, the work is pitched consistently at the ear, it abounds in similes and catalogues, it dwells on ceremonial aspects of life, and cherishes the significance of names.

Focused as it is on a small, recognizable topic, the novel is "a domestic epic" of Milkman Dead's inquiry into his family's mythic past. Thus it turns on a geneological mystery that points finally at an ancestor for this unlikely black family who is comparable to Greek and Roman heroes. But like all oral narrative, *SOS* is marked by digressions into the background and the past and present tense involvement of characters such as insurance agent Robert Smith and his grotesque attempt to fly at the novel's outset, and at Milkman's Aunt Pilate and her successful (although symbolic) flight at its end. It also digresses into discussions of the importance of place, such as the rural Pennsylvania area where Milkman's grandfather had been a farmer of nearly legendary proportion before being killed by whites.

Occasionally the rhetoric of the book is "vacant" (p.221), if one assesses style carefully, and the character Guitar is presented with a kind of "inhuman detachment" that makes him less integral than other figures.

149.   Lee, Dorothy H. "*Song of Solomon*: To Ride The Air." *BALF* 16 (1982): 64-70.

SOS is built around the story of man's archetypal search for self, for liberation, for transcendence. The four phases of the monomyth deliniate its structure: initiation, renunciation, atonement, and release (p. 64).

The book falls into two parts: the preparation (first six chapters), and the adventure. In the former, the reader gets a firm grasp of Milkman's environment, physical and familial. In the latter, he learns both about types of love from Pilate and Hagar, and types of hate from Guitar, a version of Horus, avenging son of a mutilated father.

The women's names are Biblical but ironic, as, perhaps is the sidelong allusion to the scriptural Song of Solomon in which ancestral wisdom and an understanding heart are given Solomon by God. The bulk of the incidents point readers toward Milkman's experiencing a death that leads to rebirth, as he heads into the South in search of his roots. After meeting the witch-like Circe and getting directions from her, Milkman proceeds along his Dantesque, symbolical journey to a final type of dual testing: Milkman must prove himself in the group as well as in single combat with Guitar. He is progressively divested of his old ego and reduced to being pure, unadulterated man (p. 69). Paradoxically, he learns to hunt love and to love that beast which he hunts--whether bobcat or murderous Guitar. Deep in the woods he discovers his relatives--appropriately named the Byrds--and learns to decode the song that memorializes his ancestor Solomon.

In the end, the prose operates on two levels, that of immediate reality and symbolic import. The suggestion is that Milkman's flight into expanded consciousness can be duplicated by readers.

150.   Leonard. John. "To Ride The Air To Africa." *NYT* 6 September, 1977, p.37.

Almost certainly, readers will try to pigeonhole TM's novel with restrictive labels such as its being a "Black Novel," or an important new work by a "Black Woman Novelist." But *SOS* is a book that defies confinement. The protagonist, a seeker after personal and familial truth, an epic sojourner who doesn't begin his quest for mature knowledge until he is past 30, Milkman (Macon) Dead forces the author to work through the male point of view for the first time. Milkman is shown to be constrained by his materialistic father and incredibly libidinous mother, but he is also assisted in his magical transformation into a mythic character by his Aunt Pilate. She is a kind of repository of forgotten and/or denied knowledge, a literal "pilot" for the journeying Milkman, an almost archetypal female with the capacity for literal flight. Out of Milkman's quest, presented in page upon page of mystical, even "triumphant" (p. 37) prose, comes a deepened understanding of cultural heritage.

*   Mickelson, Anne. "Winging Upward Black Women: Sarah E. Wright, Toni Morrison, Alice Walker." *Reaching Out: Sensitivity and Order in Recent American Fiction by Women.* Cited above as item 73.

151.   Millar, Neil. "Toni Morrison's brilliant black novel." *CSM* 20 October, 1977, p. 25.

The novel is a tragedy, yet it causes an affirmative magic to occur inside and outside the work. Such understanding, rage, irony, affection, and respect inform the treatment of its characters and situations that the book's love affair--which grows ecstatic and then withers into despair -causes fictional characters to grow toward charity and readers to grasp what it means to be born black in America.

Some readers might think the book anti-white because it is fired with rage and uses black myth so assertively. But in the final analysis, *SOS* makes a human statement, not a racist one.

152.   Nodelman, Perry. "The Limits of Structures: A Shorter Version of a Comparison between Toni Morrison's *Song of Solomon* and Virginia Hamilton's *M.C. Higgins The Great.*" *CLAQ* 7 (Fall, 1982): 46-48.

Although one of these novels was written for adults and the other for children, they are similar thematically. Young black men in both cases feel blocked by their fathers.

Structurally the works are different, and it is a reader's expectation about structure that tends to make the reading experience positive or negative. In fiction for children, a major premise is that characters must mature and grow up. As they develop new values, protagonists undertake a Quest (hence our expectation about form or structure in such works). The Quest causes them to leave home and subsequently to return wiser (and sometimes sadder) as a result of the loss of innocence. Such works emphasize a character's acknowledgement of the complexity of life.

In adult fiction, on the other hand, characters are already grown up, so their development of new values involves attempting to regain lost innocence. Thus for things to "get better," in adult novels, narrative situations tend to be resolved by becoming less complex.

Structurally, readers of fiction for children expect to find a unified plot, whereas readers of adult fiction expect exposition (explanations of the meaning of events). Yet *M.C. Higgins The Great* is loosely plotted, while *SOS* has an exciting plot of the "circular journey" sort typical in children's fiction. Also, because *SOS* appears to be realistic fiction yet uses fantasy extensively, it poses interpretive problems for readers who come to it with preconceptions about adult fiction.

Children need to be taught how to see and to appreciate the structural patterns of fiction.

153.   Pavelsky, Joan. "Song of Solomon." *Bookswest* 1, no.7 (February, 1978): 31.

Naming and identity are the thematic centers of this novel. Macon (Milkman) Dead is the third in his family to bear that name, one given accidentally to his grandfather by a drunk Union soldier. Women characters are also named randomly, but as a result of an odyssey into the South, the land of his ancestry, Macon explores the mystery back of his bland life and discovers a proud history of his people within which his own existence becomes meaningful.

154.   Price, Reynolds. "Black Family Chronicle." *NYT Mag* 7 (September 11, 1977): 1ff.

In her third novel, TM has been more ambitious. She deals with more characters, spins a longer prose tale, covering a century of American history, and uses fantasy, song, fable, allegory. She has a father who is intent on concealing his past, so that the son must "grow up into chaos and genuine danger" and make an "...accidental acquaintance with a ring of lifelong acquaintances who are sworn to avenge white violence, eye for eye" (p. 1).

Midway in the novel, the locale shifts abruptly, forcing Milkman to comprehend a dangerous world, but as a result to find that the world "opens into the larger, freer sphere of time and human contingency" (p. 48). The literal level of the book shifts too, almost imperceptibly, when the search for a cache of gold becomes an inquiry into the main character's family history. Although the book does not end conclusively, that is no flaw, because "no big, good novel has ever really ended" (p. 48).

155.   Rabinowitz, Paula.   "Naming, Magic and Documentary: The Subversion of Narrative in *Song of Solomon, Ceremony*, and *China Men*."   *Feminist Re-Visions: What Has Been and Might Be*.   Edited by Vivian Patraka and Louise A. Tilly.   Ann Arbor: Women's Studies Program, University of Michigan Press, 1983,   pp. 26-42.

Out of an awareness of racial difference grows a unique sense of being "other" and thus alienated psychologically, socially, politically, and culturally.   In the case of racially oppresed women, the experience is so fundamentally distinctive as to require a new language to articulate it.

TM, Leslie Marmon Silko, and Maxine Hong Kingston rework the literary techniques of majority culture by using myth, legend, and fantasy so that western literary forms blend with oral storytelling traditions of minority culture and generate a new, almost magical genre of fiction.   This genre is neither realist nor avant-garde, but instead is a type of "storytelling" in which the process of the telling (not the point of the tale) becomes the purpose.   Readers are made to interact with the tale, are engaged by the dream (or legend, joke, lore, gossip) so that a cultural truth inherent in folklore is effectively recreated.

Names in *China Men* and *SOS* show "the power of language to construct social relations and...to establish cultural history" (p. 29).   Because of its power, maintaining one's own language in naming is a way of resisting hegemonic culture and preserving identity and autonomy.

As outsiders, women cannot write a "fiction of totality" (p. 31).   Their work is always circumscribed; it tends toward the autobiographical and descriptive, using narratives which are "circular, convoluted and contextualized" (p. 31) as distinct from that which is linear and finalized.   The female personality tends to be represented in the fictions as two or more characters, and that lack of wholeness is further suggested by the fact that women characters fall into two distinct types: magical women or mundane.   The former have uncanny power, crossing the border of material reality into fantasy and myth.   The latter "maintain and reproduce life" (p. 32).   In *SOS* and *Ceremony*, magical women have a positive, life-affirming function; in *China Men* they "represent mortality and isolation" (p. 32).

Narrative technique varies.   Kingston "blurs" her use of voice by speaking as an adult woman recollecting her youthful experiences, as the young child herself, and as the objective, documentarian narrator.   Thus the reader senses an interplay among persons: the "I" and the "Other;" the insider and outsider; the participant in American culture and the observer of it.   Silko reworks Laguna myths by incorporating into sacred narrative the incidents from secular culture (prostitution in Gallup) that have affected the old ways and brought about a "recasting" of Pueblo life in the 20th century.   TM too constructs a fiction resembling history out of the voices of Milkman's "family members, friends, strangers, ghosts, and the folk tales of his culture" (p. 35).

In all three novels, the use of many voices demonstrates the fact of cultural conflict (oral/literary; male/female; hegemonic/minority) and simultaneously points to the underlying truth that for these authors, "history" is indeed a collection--even a collage--of assembled narrative fragments.

The typical westward movement of the ritual quest form, although it is used by the three women, is reversed to show the inverted experience of racial minorities. Tayo (*Ceremony*) realizes his ancestors went east and south from Asia; Milkman (*SOS*) discovers his heritage lies on the eastern seaboard and in Africa; the male figures of *China Men* travel to the east, away from their civilization, toward the "ghosts" and "demons."

Dominant American culture is pervasive in the three novels, constantly touching the characters through the popular culture (film, commercials, newspapers). Ironically, the economic exploitation of Blacks, Indians, and Chinese and the long history of their exploitation had the net effect of creating a new "race" from what were disparate groups in each case. Now through the "subversive" use of language (convoluted syntax, black idiom, the deceptive simplicity of talkstory), Morrison, Silko, and Kingston break the silence of their long alienation with literature that uses neither the language of the oppressors nor the stereotyped images of females established and maintained by patriarchal culture. The result is a genre of "magical realism" that speaks to the truth of the lived experience of women and minority readers.

156.   Rogers, Norma. "A Mockery of Afro-American Life." *Freedomways* 18 (1978): 107-09.

Skilled though TM is with language, *SOS* lacks the "substance...to nourish the mind or spirit of her readers" (p.107). Milkman Dead's supposedly deep friendship with Guitar Bains is unmotivated in the novel. They are from radically different black backgrounds, and Milkman drifts through life in his home, where his slumlord father's acquisitive personality stultifies all other members of the family into sodden passivity. The Deads are emotionally dead, and together with the family of Dr. Foster (Milkman's maternal grandparents) they represent a kind of black social arrogance and ignorance that makes one wonder whether the author has seriously examined the relation of blacks to American society generally or the complex relations within the Afro-American community.

Black women are drawn in the novel in similarly unbecoming ways. Ruth Foster Dead, First Corinthians, Magdalene--all have their dignity questioned, and their lives are shown to be "lonely, sexually deprived, mentally disturbed" (p. 108).

Nor surprisingly, Milkman prefers the company of his irrationally violent friend, Guitar, even though he cannot accept the latter's theory that "violence is a biological disease among white people" (p.108), or Guitar's consequent solution to racial violence: a random instance of violence in response to every atrocity committed against the black community.

Encouraged by Guitar, Milkman steals from his Aunt Pilate what he assumes is a sack of gold acquired years earlier when her father (his grandfather) was murdered. His search for identity in the area of his father's birth leads Milkman to the belief that his great-great-grandfather Solomon could literally fly. This enlightens Milkman, but does not clarify whether he is ultimately killed by Guitar or emulates his mythic ancestor and flies away himself.

Novelists who represent Afro-American life should work to raise reader consciousness by basing their writing on the truth of the experience. However this novel mindlessly denigrates such life.

157.   Rosenberg, Ruth. " 'And The Children May Know Their Names': Toni Morrison's *Song of Solomon*." *LOS* 8 (1981): 195-219.

This writer enjoys frustrating the critic's search for her onoma in Biblical concordances, her purpose being to force an explication of the fiction on its own terms. Naming in *SOS* corresponds to historical fact (TM's mother, Rahmah, having been named in the same fashion as some of the characters), and thus invites a sociological reading of the sort which sees the novel's names as representing the changing status of blacks in American society.

The first category of names employed includes those which suggest locality or self-image or chronology, and which (as in the case of TM's mother and First Corinthians) may be "picked blind." The second category consists of post-Civil War rural southern (sometimes called "nigger") names. The third is made up of names imposed by white officialdom ("colored" names) as blacks migrated to northern cities in the first half of the 20th century. The last category is the group of black militant names growing out of the civil rights movement of the sixties and designed to reject European colonialization.

Simply put, the novel's theme is the human ability to transcend circumstances. This is dramatized by the metaphor of flight and is represented onomastically in Pilate's cross-generated name, although the book's major focus is on Macon Dead III's shedding his "nigger" name and recovering for himself the magical name of his ancestor Solomon, appropriately derived from a Canaanite deity meaning "completion, fulfillment." Milkman's discarding the designation "dead" for his true name completes his final rebirth--by African tradition he is a thing, an "it" until truly named--removes his oedipal limp, and rejoins him into the kinship of his family group. Ironically, the most militant of characters in the novel are not freed by their names or activities, but instead become more enslaved by hatred than they ever were by colonial masters.

158.   Royster, Philip M. "Milkman's Flying: The Scapegoat Transcended in Toni Morrison's *Song of Solomon*" *CLAJ* 24 (1980): 419-40.
        Because its narrative traces the growth of the protagonist's personal identity, *SOS* is a version of Bildungsroman. Basically Milkman has to grow through his scapegoat-victim role and be reconciled to the social order. His scapegoat-victim role began even before his birth, when his father tried to abort his mother's foetus. It continues through childhood and his love affair with Hagar, is extended in a fight in Shalimar, Virginia, and climaxed when his lifelong friend, Guitar, tries to kill him.
        His awareness of his scapegoat-victim role begins when he first meets Pilate. Her singing and storytelling stimulate his transformation and provoke his inquiry into his family's past. What stands in his way is his ignorance--ignorance of women and love, ignorance of work, ignorance of the violent tensions between parents, ignorance of the existence of choice, ignorance of the world at large. Unknowing as he is and lacking control of his own life, Milkman is an unwilling, helpless victim of others (p. 431) both white and black.
        In Montour County, PA, the site of his grandfather's farm, and subsequently in Shalimar, VA, the birthplace of his family, Milkman learns self-reliance and comes in contact with the resources of his Afro-American culture. The recurring metaphor for his acquired knowledge is the act of flying: "transcendence is the central activity of the novel" (p. 438). His epiphany costs his mentor, Pilate, her life, but she too has been a scapegoat outcast. In the end he is deeply aware of both how to live and how to die/fly.

159.   Samuels, Wilfrid D. "Liminality and the Search For Self in Toni Morrison's *Song of Solomon*." *MV* 5 (Spring-Fall, 1981): 59-68.
        The essay adopts Houston A. Baker's theory of viewing literature as a type of cultural anthropology. First Milkman's birth, childhood, and manly quest are likened to the archetypal career of a traditional hero. Then an extended analysis of his life follows, done according to the terms and concepts of Arnold van Gennep's *Rites of Passage*. At issue is the assertion that Milkman exists in a "liminal" or marginal condition in his rite of passage from adolescence to adulthood. His birth bears ritual marks of his being a "dead" (Dead) character. Throughout his youth he lives outside the community and outside his family. Even his important initiatory sexual relationship with Hagar is, by virtue of being incestuous, an indication of his being "polluted."
        He has no sense of the collective solidarity of people. But guided by the mysterious Pilate (in the role of griot), Milkman

undergoes a series of physical and psychological trials in isolation in Pennsylvania and Virginia which cleanse him and even transform him from insubstantial limbo-figure into a full-fledged member of the African community descended from the flying Solomon. His discovery of self is at the same time an acknowledgement of his incorporation into a cultural group and the completion of his rite of passage.

160. Scruggs, Charles. "The Nature of Desire in Toni Morrison's *Song of Solomon.*" *ArQ* 38 (Winter, 1982): 311-35.
Their "desires"--yearnings for love, sex, gold, roots, vengeance--are what make Morrison's characters unusual. They may be fulfilled by such yearnings, or they may also become distorted into "grotesques," because by itself, without attendant wisdom, desire cannot lead characters out of what Plato terms "the cave."
Just as in *The Symposium*, there is in *SOS* a ladder of love, a hierarchy of lovers by which Morrison evaluates her characters. One type of desire makes characters rise above their humanity, another causes them to sink beneath its weight. Macon (Jake) Dead desired personal independence achieved through ownership and love of farmland. His son, Macon Junior, desires only gold and is thus trapped in Mammon's cave. Pilate desires the spiritual peace that comes from setting her father's ghost at rest and becoming part of a community. Ruth yearns so deeply to be loved, to be freed from the prison of self wherein she is pressed small, that she expresses her needs through vengeance and incestuous impulses. Her daughter First Corinthians also desires to be freed by love, and finds that salvation in Porter, at one time a member of the Seven Days hate group. Another irony is evident in that Guitar says he wants to love black people, but his entire life is committed to vengeful killing, even of his best friend.
The novel's central figure, Milkman, thinks that he desires gold (as does his father), but winds up discovering the much more important value of being connected to one's community and one's past. Unlike his murderous brother Guitar, Milkman learns to love individuals and in so doing comprehends--ever so briefly--man's potential for transcendence.

161. Smith, Valerie A. "'The Singer in One's Soul': Storytelling in the Fiction of James Weldon Johnson, Richard Wright, Ralph Ellison, and Toni Morrison." Ph.D. diss., University of Virginia, 1982. *DAI* 43 (1982): 2350.
Four novels by Afro-American writers (*Autobiography of An Ex-Colored Man; Native Son; Invisible Man; SOS*) treat the quest for personal identity. Protagonists in each work discover that the ordering power of language affords them philosophical freedom.

Being able to tell one's own story implies gaining self-knowledge, and it also effectively frees the characters from oppressive white history. The storyteller's personal version of his story replaces "a destructive, linear sense of time with a regenerative, cyclic conception" (p. 2350) that provides individual authenticity and control over time. Milkman, in particular, gains emotional strength when he learns the song/story of his family.

162. "Song of Solomon." *KR* 45 (July 1, 1977): 686.

Milkman Dead is radically isolated from his family, unloved by them and unloving. But finally he begins a "cleansing Odyssean journey' which forces him to pass through transforming landscapes and confront ghostly tales that illuminate the history of his family. He must deal meaningfully with eerie and wise old characters such as Circe, and even with the deceptive simplicity of children whose games preserve remnants of the past and prophecy the future. As a process of undergoing this journey, Milkman becomes an emblem for the many black persons who must retrieve their identity from the past in order to be free from the "no-name state of /their/ forebears" (p.686). Once liberated from his burdensome past, Milkman does achieve the capacity to love.

163. Taliaferro, Frances. "Books in Brief: *Song of Solomon.*" *Harpers* 255 (October, 1977): 94.

This novel is distinguished from Morrison's earlier work by being more ambitious, even though the material she treats is a "traditional" rites of passage type. Milkman Dead is forced from his easy, "cushioned" life and made to undergo a series of ritual tests as he pursues self-knowledge and earns his way "into the tribe of adults" (p.94). The novel is wise, rich, and sensuous.

164. Tate, Claudia C. "The Song of Solomon." *CLAJ* 21 (December, 1977): 327-29.

Young Macon (Milkman) Dead is estranged from his family in an almost archtypically adolescent way: he is disinterested in them and totally focused on himself. Intelligently structured as it is, the novel maneuvers events so that Milkman can escape from the entanglements of family only by immersing himself in its past history. When he does, and more deeply than he had imagined possible, he comes to "revere his once despised heritage," and at the untimely end of his life he achieves his own and his grandfather's singular ambition by "soaring spiritually from duress" (p. 328).

TM's preceding books were built upon lyrical prose, subtly disclosed narrative, "melodic dialogue," and a profound interest in character portrayal. *SOS,* on the other hand, is like a mystery story.

Its emphasis rests on intrigue, on "revelation of mysterious past events," on assembling clues that lead logically toward the all important narrative climax. It is a book which tells us quite explicitly what happened, whereas the earlier novels suggested how characters lived. The distinction may seem slight, yet it makes this latest work--densely plotted and more lengthy though it be--a slighter achievement.

165.   Wegs, Joyce. "Toni Morrison's *Song of Solomon*: A Blues Song." *EILWIU* 9 (1982): 211-23.
    Taking as a cue TM's reference in an interview with Thomas LeClair (see III.26 above) to her function as a creator of "peasant literature" for her community and hence an equivalent of the old singers of blues, Wegs analyzes that blues-like function in *SOS*. There the men tend to "fly away" from harsh experience. Robert Smith attempts his suicidal flight from the roof of Mercy Hospital as he seeks forgiveness for his part in The Days, a secret society devoted to a brutal kind of "justice" through murder. His failed flight provokes the first singing of the blues tune about Sugarman (Solomon), thus linking soaring and song early in the work. Even Milkman himself flies away from Michigan to Pennsylvania and abandons the grieving Hagar to her blues. At the same time, staying at home, as does Macon Dead II, produces sodden misery too, and provides a context for the blues as Ruth would know them. In Milkman's grandfather's generation the pattern is broken: Macon Dead (Jake) stays determinedly with his family, having been left alone with children at his wife's untimely death, and after he is murdered, his ghost too refuses to leave. Macon stays in place, it is suggested, because he has the kind of "dominion" over land which TM noted in the LeClair interview as typically denied black males. Thus old Jake becomes a model of the ideal father figure for Morrison.
    The novel traces Milkman's gradually becoming a genuine "blues man," first finding his own identity, then learning a sense of community with his people. That learning is effected through his understanding of a children's playground game based on the collective memory of the exploits of Milkman's great-grandfather, Solomon, who the story says, flew away from his wife and 20 children, attempting to take only the youngest, Jake, with him.
    That myth of flight is the sort of culturally sustaining material which TM aims to recover and preserve for her people. It exists in multiple versions, one unbecoming because it has all the males simply fly off, another more positive and communal in that it concerns an elderly man who helps others in the community to remember their power and to fly off "like...crows" from oppression (p. 218).
    At the same time, much of TM's novel is implicitly critical of men for their selfishness, childishness, and desire for domination. The mentor who takes charge of Milkman's outgrowing such negative

traits is his Aunt Pilate. A genuine blues-man, he learns, is never going it solo, but is connected "musically" to others.

In fairness, it should be noted that TM is critical of black women too. Her chief spokesman for that assessment of women is Guitar, an ambiguous figure in his own right, but a persuasive purveyor of the notion that black women are smotheringly possessive even though they disguise that "anaconda love" as domesticity (p. 220). Not many women have the selfless sense of strength of Pilate, who knew intimately the value of community and the need to act upon love. As she dies, with Milkman, the emerging blues-man, singing for her, Pilate's name flies away in the beak of a bird, and then Milkman soars after her.

166. Wigan, Angela. "Native Daughter." *Time* 12 September, 1977, p.76ff.

With *SOS,* Morrison achieves the kind of combined breadth of personal and cultural vision which marks the fifth stage of black American writing: "a wider vision of the world" (p. 76). Preceding evolutionary stages include 1) protest, 2) reflective search for personal identity, 3) exploration of culture, and 4) refinement of craft.

This novel is a family history spanning the time from the Civil War to the civil rights movement, and chronicling the rise of the upwardly mobile Dead family from slavery to middle class respectability. Milkman Dead is stuffed with material things but starved for knowledge of his heritage. His dream is to fly (i.e., to be released from bondage imaginatively). He realizes that dream with the aid of his outcast Aunt Pilate. She is a storehouse of magic, voodoo and history, and nourished by her life, Milkman discovers the mythic secret of his slave-grandfather, still preserved and being ritually repeated in a children's playground game in Virginia.

The novel is certain to be compared to *Roots,* but that simple, analagous assertion once granted, *SOS* gives clear evidence of the considerable achievement of Morrison's art.

167. Winslow, Henry F., Sr. "Book Corner: *Song of Solomon.*" *Crisis* 85 (March, 1978): 105-06.

Milkman Dead is the protagonist of the novel, but he is upstaged consistently by his resourceful Aunt Pilate, a model of "authentic womanhood" (p. 105). Pilate earned her independence as a walker and a worker in the world, and she has resolutely clung to her memory of her father's being murdered by greedy whites wanting his profitable farm. Most distinctively of all, Pilate remains gently forgiving and almost totally unmaterialistic, contrary to her acquisitive brother (Milkman's father), Macon.

When Milkman defends his mother by aggressively (and archetypally) confronting his father, Macon needles the young man by revealing his own nastiest suspicions about his wife's lifelong, unnatural attachment to her father. Ruth responds by telling her son her version of the truth. Thus provoked by contradiction, Milkman sets out on a literal odyssey in search of his roots. Milkman believes he is searching for gold, a treasure that his father has taught him will set him free. He discovers instead one of the primary lessons of western humanist literature: love of money is the root of all evil; it is also power, but power that corrupts, even absolutely (p. 106).

Morrison's work consistently treats the lives of men and women entangled in their weaknesses. In *SOS* her protagonist triumphs over such shortcomings.

PART V
CRITICISM OF SPECIFIC WORKS: *TAR BABY*

168.   Bell, Pearl K. "Self-Seekers." *Commentary* 72, no. 2 (August, 1981): 56-60 n.

TB belongs to the class of fiction concerned with the struggle to find one's identity and choose one's own destiny. A principal problem of such material involves allowing individuals to define their uniqueness without weakening ties to institutions which place limits on the definition.

Here, Jadine's affirmation of her individuality ("not black--just me") forces her to deny her heritage in the black culture (p. 56). Customarily black authors are not concerned with psychological reality; social realities are challenging enough. For TM too this novel is a departure from her erstwhile preoccupation with isolated black neighborhoods and women "disfigured by helplessness" (p. 57).

TB has a disjointed quality, its setting on a French island in the Caribbean producing "florid language, incongruous parts, a doomed love story and a particularly harsh indictment of white civilization" (p. 57). The erratic portrait of Valerian and the novel's lack of symbolic breadth and substance prevent *TB* from being "the microcosm of white civilization she seems to have in mind" (p. 57).

The racial and cultural tension which grow out of Jadine's and Son's love affair is unequally weighted on Son's side. He is too clearly the author's noble savage whose firm sense of self is capable of redeeming Jadine. Committed as she has been all along to the notion of women as culture bearers, TM apparently has no sympathy for Jadine's offense against the race and herself. Hers is the great sacrilege; she has forfeited her tribal soul to white learning and culture.

The reviewer believes TM herself is ambivalent about her subject, and the result is a disquieting lushness about the prose that is either pointlessly extravagant or grotesque, particularly in the author's "incessant anthropomorphizing of nature" (p. 57).

Bell's is one of few voices raised in criticism of the "garbled" application of the tar baby story. In Uncle Remus, the tar baby is a black doll placed by the white farmer to catch the rabbit in the cabbage patch. Yet as applied by Son in the book's climactic quarrel, the story would make Valerian the white man who creates tar baby Jadine. "How, then, does Son stand for the rabbit who outsmarts the farmer and runs away? Why does he desperately try to find Jadine after she runs back to Paris? None of this makes much sense" (p. 57).

169.   Brown, Rosellen. "Grits and Grace." *NY* 14 (April 13, 1981): 42.
       White characters figure much more prominently in TM's latest
work, but they do so as oppressors. Slavery continues in *TB* with a
significant shift in emphasis: blacks are in cultural bondage, not
economic or political. In the Caribbean island household of retired
candy manufacturer Valerian Street and his neurotic wife Margaret,
three coopted blacks shuffle along in their respective ways. Sydney
and Ondine are the servants to the Streets who have acquiesced to their
bondage in an effort to assure themselves a slice of the good life, and
who, in the privacy of their own rooms, not unexpectedly despise
their benefactor-employers bitterly. Jadine, their high yellow niece,
has allowed her inner self to be "purchased" by Valerian at the price of
a first-class European education that has "transformed white culture
into the very cells of /her/ memory" (p. 42).
       To generate temptation and to force the cultural clash on which
her book is focused, TM brings into the island's insulated
environment a propertyless, renegade black man who terrifies both the
older couples, black and white, and arouses conflicting passions in
Jadine. She and the emblematically named "Son" are quickly
embroiled in a values dogfight from which only one can emerge.
       The fiction is overrich in thematic invention, and so its impact is
diffuse. Issues related to maternity, and to the responsibilities of
"culture-bearing black women," and to models and types of black
manhood all abound. Apparently TM is engaged in the process of
creating new myths, yet as author she locates herself outside her
material and from there judges and scolds the characters rather than
announcing them prophetically and allowing their mystery as genuine,
complexly human figures to predominate.

170.   Broyard, Anatole. "Two-Way Protest." *NYT* 21 March, 1981, p. 10.
       A novel as well written as the prize winning *SOS* (1978 National
Book Critics Circle Award) leads one to expect high quality fiction in
the author's next effort. That expectation is unsatisfied. *TB* is poorly
crafted. Its characters are presented with unconvincing racial bias, its
meaning is obscure, and its effect is to produce alienation between
black and white readers, instead of bringing all elements of the reading
public together to communicate about fiction.

171.   Caplan, Brina. "A Fierce Conflict of Colors." *Nat* 232 (May 2, 1981):
       529-30 ff.
       Usually TM manipulates the storyteller's art to reveal the isolated
but richly complex black cultures that exist within hostile white
society. In that aim and in her use of folklore to effect it, the author is
like Isaac Bashevis Singer. But neither the presentation of community

nor the function of folklore is effectively engaging in *TB*, because the book's "messages," its concerns for making statements about race, class, and culture, turn it into a ponderous novel of ideas. Characters become spokespersons for representative opinions and are with disturbing frequency merely sketched in two dimensions. Structural devices necessary to carry the weight of the message (paired conversations, contrapuntal scenes, symbolism of color, allegory, symbolism of place and name) are obtrusive instead of integral to the fiction.

This time the community TM deals with is itself displaced and shot through with strife instead of being mutually supportive, as in her earlier work. Valerian and Margaret Street exploit their black servants as they have done to the Caribbean workers who built their artificial hideaway. Seen up close, Margaret is a compulsive child-abuser, and wealthy, apparently urbane Valerian is a "moral blank" whose "sin is willful unknowing" of his wife's domestic violence (p. 529).

The aristocratic control over people's lives exercised by the Streets is shattered by the arrival on the island of a "natural" black man, Son Green. His conflict with Valerian is TM's way of presenting the struggle between "industry" values and "fraternal" ones (p. 530). Son's passionate, sexual involvement with Jadine diminishes for a time her sense that she is "inauthentic," but her acquired taste and deep need for the high culture of New York City ("a black woman's town," p. 530) and Paris is irreconcilable with Son's for earthy, rural Florida and its attendant values. In that down-home setting the conservative understanding of sex roles and behavior, especially as applied to women, terrify Jadine. She fears her future is threatened if she commits herself to him; he feels his past is eroded by her. That abiding opposition between them is not resolved in the end.

Revealed in the fiction is the fact that TM does not believe in the romantic notion that an individual has the capacity to become whatever he/she wishes. To the contrary: genuine human identity is derived from connections, from "shared values, patterns of obligation and cooperation" (p.534). Lacking that sense of cultural community, one becomes merely a thing.

172. Christian, Barbara. "Testing The Strength of The Black Cultural Bond: Review of Toni Morrison's *Tar Baby*." *Black Feminist Criticism*. New York, Oxford, Toronto, Sydney, Paris, Frankfurt: Athene Series, Pergamon Press, 1981, pp. 65-69 (Reprinted from *In These Times*, 14 July, 1981).

TM extends the folk tale of the tar baby into a "contemporary fable"(p. 66). Wealthy candy manufacturer, Valerian Street, rules imperialistically over the inhabitants of the Caribbean island he's retired to, as well as over his much younger wife, and two industrious, socially conscious "Philadelphia Negroes" who are his servants. Jadine, the tar baby, is the orphaned niece of these servants, an Afro-American Princess myopically committed to making it in the modern, western world. Her sense of self is badly shaken when an "authentic" African woman spits at her in Paris, so she flees to the island to recover and reflect.

The isolated, placid lifestyle of the island is disrupted by the arrival of a fugitive black man named Son who becomes the rabbit of the tale. Son agitates Valerian and Margaret and even Sydney and Ondine, whom he exposes as "classist" blacks. His sexuality excites and terrifies Jadine (who fears losing control), but more importantly, it is the clash between her "individualistic, materialistic" drives and Son's passion for his roots, for chauvinistic behavior, and for insisting upon woman-as-nurturer that dominates the book.

TM raises the very problematical question "whether there is a functional black culture in the present-day West" (p. 68). By implication, the answer given by *TB* is no, because Jadine opts for the merits of Paris and western culture, while Son drops away into the misty world of legendary island horsemen, an image of the past that has no relevance for or impact on this age. The author here uses and thus examines the uncomfortable relevance of certain stereotypical concepts and characters: the cliched but false suggestion that when enslaved, house servants and field servants separated themselves; the suggestion that house slaves were female, field slaves male. An accurate reading of the book points to the vexing conclusion that "stereotypes that were not true 100 years ago have now become reality" (p.69). If TM is correct, blacks are worse off now than in their oppressive slave past.

173.   Domowitz, Janet. "An intricate tale of power, tension." *CSM* 13 April, 1981, p. B 3.

A complex web of tensions is woven between white millionaire Valerian Street and the Sorbonne-educated niece of his lifelong black servants. Through the master's patronage, Jadine Childs has become a Parisian model and a repository of western culture. When she falls in love with a black American fugitive who swims ashore on Valerian's Caribbean paradise, both gender and racial conflicts are dramatized in their stormy relationship.

In this book, TM shows how divergent have been the black responses to what has been termed a "common black experience" (p. B 3). Especially keen is TM's presentation of the struggle between the black man (immature, mama-spoiled) and black woman (culture-bearing, but whose culture?). That conflict is not triumphantly resolved.

174.   Donavin, Denise P.   "Tar Baby." *Booklist* 77 (January 15, 1981), p.650.

TM repeats, in this latest work, her strategy of using mythology as she did in *SOS*. West Indian myths here undergird her contemporary story of ideological and gender conflict between an earthy black man (Son Green) and the worldly, leisured woman who is his opposite (Jadine Childs). All the novel's characters might have maintained their mindless lives of accommodation had not Son appeared in their island hideaway to stir up personal anguish, gender hostility, and racial friction.

175.   Erickson, Peter B. "Images of Nurturance in Toni Morrison's *Tar Baby*." *CLAJ* 28 (1984): 11-32.

Critical opinion of *TB* has tended to stress its difference from TM's earlier work, but in fact the latest novel simply extends her recurring concern with maternal sexuality and generational continuity among black women. Using a reverse strategy, the author focuses her theme in *TB* by showing disconnections among the principal black women--Therese, Ondine, and Jadine. The latter, for instance, achieves an independence denied Sula, but does so at such a cost as to come across negatively to a reader.

Two mysterious boy children drive the narrative forward, one the fugitive Son who dominates the Streets' household, the other Michael, their biological son who never appears. Together they illustrate the theme of failed nurturance buried at the core of the novel and dramatized both in terms of mothering and of food. Margaret is a perversion of motherhood, Valerian the archetypal absent father preoccupied by business for the first 30 years of his child's life and now mummified in his retirement greenhouse. Ondine comforts Michael after his mother abuses him, but she too fails significantly: she says nothing about the abuse.

All this is background for Jadine's struggle against maternity. Her vision of maternity is frightening, a tar baby she must avoid at all costs. Both the swamp of the Caribbean island and the black society of Eloe, Florida, threaten Jadine with a vision of femaleness she perceives as oppressive. Her defiance of conventional expectation extends the notion of dissolution of neighborhood ideas begun with Sula's institutionalizing her grandmother. Jadine's rejection of Sydney and Ondine is analogous to her leaving Son: both stand for the "threat of orthodox motherhood" (p. 21), but in so doing she inverts the Sula-Jude relationship of the earlier book. Now it is the woman who takes the initiative, breaks the relationship, and leaves.

Although the author is characteristically generous in her portrait of the pathetic Margaret, she is unnecessarily harsh on Jadine. The latter is held up as a target for those who value black culture, and her sexuality is sketched as superficial and unsympathetic (p. 24). While the connection between Son and the symbolical Therese grows, Jadine is debased even more. Therese insists Son become a legendary male and in the process abandon forever this woman who "has forgotten her ancient properties" (p.27). Besides the flaw in the book that comes from convicting Jadine, TM further weakens the work by romanticizing the mythology of black male flight and by stubbornly refusing to allow motherhood to be read positively in the book.

176. Falk, Richard. "Fables For Our Times: Six Novels." *YR* 71 (Winter, 1982): 254ff.

Some recent fiction, perhaps springing from values bases similar to John Gardner's (*On Moral Fiction*), reveals a tendency to disavow that pervasive gloom which has marked writing for much of the past century. Instead of flaunting fashionable pessimism, notable new works are being created with a "larger sense of life and a more epic scale of human virtue and vice..." (p. 255). This represents a kind of artistic return to beauty and moral order in hopes that the rest of the world will follow.

TB is set in a primitive, magical landscape where both the white and black inhabitants of the Caribbean island are wrestling with their respective ghosts. TM's fiction is spun from the stuff of folktales but lacking in the naturalness and the believability of folk material. Her prose is too often precious, and her characterizations are diminished by her use of pathetic fallacy (of Son, she writes, "...he saw the stars...and exchanged stares with the moon...").

She appears not to believe her own material and to be attempting to flesh it out with rhetorical flourishes. Consequently dramatic conflict is set out in easy, even stereotypical terms. The white world is totally out of touch with nature and thus subject to a variety of dismal failings, including being poor parents. On the other hand, the nonwhite world is attuned to the natural, hence those women are still women and the men still men--though what that appears to mean, in practice, is that they "know how to bully and neglect /the women/" (p. 260).

Sometimes, as in a scene which occurs in Son's native Florida, the writing is accurate and lively, but for the most part the book is not a novel so much as "a diagram of a novel" (p. 260). What should be realized in fictional terms (characters, plot) is overwhelmed by the messages it must carry.

177. Fishman, Charles. "Naming Names: Three Recent Novels by Women Writers." *Names* 32 (1984): 33-44.

Alice Walker (*Meridian*, 1976), Margaret Atwood (*Life Before Man*, 1979) and TM (*TB*, 1981) all use names and naming in ways which are both denotative and symbolical. Fishman proposes five functional categories for such naming:

I. Names Indicating Levels and Boundaries. These may make clear distinctions, or they may suggest layered, ambiguous, and even mythic meanings, as do place names in *TB*. Son's route through the

Caribbean landscape (Isle de Chevaliers, L'Arbe de la Croix, Sein de Vielles) and thence to his edenic birthplace in Florida (Eloe/Elohim) and back is a mythic journey of personal revelation.

II. Names Indicating Class or Status. Economic class impacts significantly on naming. White property owners use generic names such as "Yardman, the gardner," or "Mary" to dehumanize entire classes of persons who work for them.

III. Names Indicating Barriers. Purposefully attaching dehumanizing labels removes respect for persons as individuals. Sydney and Ondine become "Kingfish and Beulah" to Margaret Street, and she herself in turn becomes "The Principal Beauty of Maine...the main bitch of the prince" to Ondine (p. 37). This kind of labeling may be unintentional misnaming, as when Jade is called "Son's Northern girl," or calculatedly degrading, as when Son thinks of Jade as "house-bitch...corporate cunt, tar baby, side-of-the-road whore trap" and when Margaret flings her guilty anger back at Ondine, screaming, "Shut up! Shut up! You nigger! You nigger bitch!" (p. 38).

IV. Names Indicating Real and/or Imaginary Power. Names have a magical, transformative power that gives the namer control by virtue of the knowledge of names.

V. Names Indicating Roots of Identity. Because labeling, if desirable, can lend dignity and power, characters such as Son (William Green) are deeply immersed in the search for "the original name" (p. 41) that is equated with spiritual wholeness. What is sought in the quest for one's original name is no less than the meaning of one's history, realizable in the symbolical recovery of "what /one/ had at the start of ... life" (p. 42).

178.   Hill, Lynda. "An Island, A Vision, The Beauty, and Son." *BlEnt* 11 July, 1981, p. 13.

Conflict between an authentic Brer Rabbit (the stowaway, Son) and an inauthentic tar baby (Jadine Childs) is derived from familiar folklore neatly applied to realistic contemporary life. Yet despite such relevance, *TB* is "mostly fantasy," its setting a fictional Caribbean island, its tone "more humorous than any of Morrison's past novels" (p. 13). This time around TM strings together narrative episodes neither bizarre nor menacing, as has been her wont. Thus this most recent fiction takes the reader away from familiar TM territory and onto new ground that will require close study. The lyrical, sensual style and the deeply human understanding of the author are both present as always in this new book. TM must be ranked, in terms of the critical recognition already afforded her, ahead of all other black female writers except perhaps Lorraine Hansberry, and right alongside James Baldwin, Ralph Ellison, and Richard Wright.

144

179.   Horan, Michael F. "Tar Baby." *Best Sellers* 41 (June, 1981): 90.
        Out of the initial hostility between high-cultured Jadine Childs
and the ignorant "swamp Nigger" Son Green grows a kind of self-
awareness that allows these characters to see themselves as
complementary opposites. TM's tale reveals the threatening violence
in some black men as well as the extent to which certain black women
have sold out their heritage to gain worldly success. So powerful and
so deep are the cultural, racial, and sexual differences between people
that only a treatment in mythological terms such as TM has used here
can do the subject justice.

180.   House, Elizabeth B. "Toni Morrison." *DLB Yearbook, 1981.* Edited
        by Karen L. Rood, Jean W. Ross and Richard Ziegfeld. Detroit,
        Michigan: Gale Research Company, 1982, pp. 114-19.
        TB marks two significant changes in TM's approach to her
subject. It uses exotic locales instead of the small midwestern towns
of her earlier work, and it involves white characters as central to the
conflict.
        Learning to accommodate the cultural past in one's present is the
major content issue of the novel. Its form is an updated version of the
tar baby folktale which has as its enticing trap the alluring high fashion
black model Jadine Childs. In the process of earning (and being
given) success in white, European culture, Jadine has lost touch with
her heritage and feels empty and "inauthentic" personally.
        Conflict erupts when all the rules of social propriety are broken,
most notably by the renegade "Son" Green, who drifts into and then
disrupts the apparently serene lives of the island families. In
addition, the real son of Valerian and Margaret Street has been
psychologically damaged by his mother, and now disrupts her plans
and his father's with his rejection of their lifestyle. Even Jadine's
foster parents fear, at their deepest emotional level, that she will
disrupt their lives by abandoning them at the end of their lives when
they need her most.
        In short, as bonds between parents and children dissolve, what
occurs is general cultural decay. Writ small in the lives of her half
dozen characters, TM chronicles the crumbling of social order through
various abuses of power.
        No happy ending is possible, given this novel's subtle and
tangled complications. The passionate love affair between Jadine and
Son is not compelling enough to overcome the radical differences in
their respective definitions of themselves and in what each seeks in a
mate. Herein the novel deals with what it means to be a "man" and a
"woman."
        Critical response to *TB* has been deeply divided. Originality of
characterization, engaging use of voice, stunning description of place
are TM's assets in the book. Weaknesses include its overwritten
narrative construction and its occasionally precious tone. That she

concerns herself with the most pervasive of mankind's problems--"the human heart in conflict with itself" (p. 118)--argues eloquently for this author's continuing growth.

181.   Howard, Maureen. "A Novel of Exile and Home." *NRep* 184 (March 21, 1981): 29-32.
        Novelist Howard admires the way TM seems to have a complete and detailed dossier on every character in her fiction; thus Howard assesses *TB* in terms of myth or black history or narrative structure, rather than by commenting on the subtle complexity of the dossiers of principal figures. They occupy a Haitian island that is idyllic, magical (the very flora and fauna are alive and comment on the action of the book), and menacing. Into their complacent, idly rich, bored, inauthentic lives comes not Michael--the estranged son of Valerian and Margaret Street--but a "black American prince" (p. 30) appropriately named Son. His arrival shifts the novel into high gear and a psychologically harrowing series of revelations occurs. Ultimately the Streets settle into an uneasy form of penance for past sins, and the power shifts clearly from them to their lifelong black servants.
        A flawed section of the novel is that which treats Jade's and Son's trip to New York and then to his home in Florida, searching for a place where they can settle down to love each other. The section is not credible; characters "talk too much" and "are talked about too much" (p. 30), the novel becoming a dull commentary on black men and women instead of dramatically realized fiction.
        The novel reverts in its ending to fable. Son is advised by a blind island woman to choose a wild, natural condition on the Isle des Chevaliers instead of civilized life with Jadine. When he runs off "lickety-split" like the rabbit of the tar baby tale, Son does seem to be returning to a natural state and a childish world of magic. But the novel for all its use of fantasy is a highly realistic presentation of the ambiguity in which we all must live and act.

182.   Huth, Angela. "Electric Rubens." *List* 106 (December 17, 1981): 793.
        TB is contrasted (to its disadvantage) with novels by three contemporary English women novelists. All treat dilemmas in "small worlds" as is characteristic of Jane Austen, but TM's particular world is "a cardboard Caribbean island" (p. 793) peopled by banal character types. She has not "mastered subtlety of exposition" (p.793).

183.   Irving, John. "Morrison's Black Fable." *NYTBR* 29 March, 1981, pp. 1, 30-31.
        Irving chides TM gently at the outset for betraying the characteristic weaknesses of all great writers: doing to excess what they do well. Specifically for TM this means allowing herself to be

uncritically and excessively self-indulgent with her prose. That forgivable flaw shows up in her inclination to "mythologize her characters as soon as they're born" (p.30). Looking back at her earlier work, Irving sees frequent evidence of wryly amused mythologizing: Mercy Hospital called No Mercy by the blacks; a black culture-bearer named Pilate, born with no navel; in a town called Medallion, a black community occupies an area called The Bottom, and annually celebrates National Suicide Day.

Now in *TB* , TM creates a lush Caribbean setting within which a wealthy white candy manufacturer, Valerian Street, his wife Margaret, and their black cook and butler intend to crawl away dreamily toward death. TM's penchant for irony shows clearly in the fact that Sydney and Ondine, the black couple, are morally superior because they know and are willing to face up to a cruel truth about their employers. The Streets are rigorously repressing that truth. The irony is deepened by the fact that the Street's son Michael does not return to the island home for Christmas, but a singular black man named Son, an escaped convict from Florida, does. With his appearance, whatever equilibrium existed in the lives of the four older characters is radically upset.

Valerian Street can no longer retreat from his particular realities into his fetid greenhouse. Margaret, his wife, cannot embalm herself in indolent housekeeping. Sydney and Ondine cannot maintain their carefully preserved facade of being "good Negroes." And most importantly, Sydney and Ondine's niece, Jadine, an incredibly lovely, well-educated Paris model, cannot continue unprovoked in her assumption that she can live quite contentedly and comfortably, thank you, among upper class whites.

TM deals with a variety of racial tensions, and it is to her credit that she courageously dramatizes such tensions as sharply present among the black characters. Even to Sydney and Ondine, Son is "just a swamp nigger" (p. 30). The divisive, ongoing debate among cultured, affluent blacks about whether to accommodate themselves to white society is presented somewhat tediously by the conflict between Jadine and Son. She shows him her beloved New York City, and he finds it full of hypocrites. He then takes her to rural Florida to show her "real" blacks, and she is bored and repulsed. Jadine flees to Europe and to wealth, finally, and Son loses himself in search of her in the island's swamps, returning, as it were, to "a powerfully syperstitious...culture, radically different from the culture of black America" (p. 31).

Her major accomplishment here is to have written a woman's book, a black book, a socially realistic book, and to have raised this work by virtue of her great talent to the level of being broadly symbolical of universal human issues growing out of race and gender.

Weaknesses are evident in the novel for all to see. One is its excessive reliance on dialogue, which produces tedium. Related to that is the author's inclination to personify nature in her descriptions in terms that border on being precious. Structurally the overlapping narrative is "an irritation" (p.31), and the calculatedly "open," mythological conclusion may be unnecessarily opaque on the narrative level.

In the final analysis, Irving applauds the vision of TM's work, its thematic ambition ("the vast discrepancies between the places black people end up and the places they seek"), and above all its Hardyesque moral judgements, sympathetic as well as severe, on "damaged mankind" (31).

184. Jackson, Marni. "Rich imaginings, queenly sadness." *Mac* 94 (April 27, 1981): 59-60.

Fiction is, in contrast with film or television, a private medium accessible only with the expenditure of unique effort by the audience. TM's fourth novel demands of readers both an investment of trust and an effort of imagination. Into an exotic Caribbean setting which functions as the stage for a situation of "civilized black-and-white-detente" (p. 59) comes the Disruptive Stranger of 19th century fiction who ignites a series of personal and racial explosions. The love affair between Son, the undocumented, illiterate black stranger, and Jadine, a prototype of the chic black businesswoman, is the novel's center. Both racial culture and social history are invested in their passionate conflict, because hanging in balance is the value placed by characters and reader in one's education, in color, and in gender. A multitude of relationships crowd the book: blacks to others less black; blacks to whites; men to women; women to women; mothers to sons; and people to nature.

Although it exhibits a tendency to melodrama, the novel is kept under TM's strict authorial control. She never loses sight of her commitment to make every detail in it mean something. Finally one wonders, in fact, whether she is not too self-conscious about her role as author, too aware of her ability to write "like the black Faulkner of New York" (p. 60).

185. Kubal, David. "Fiction Chronicle: *Tar Baby*." *HudR* 34 (Autumn, 1981): 463-65.

This book treats the "deterioration of black relationships" (p. 463) in no uncertain terms. TM appears to despair of any real relationship between black men and black women. Both struggle to free themselves from whatever "tar baby" threatens to enmesh and destroy them, but as the women proceed alone into the world, "the men return to a mythical past, beyond culture" (p. 463).

Seen whole, *TB* concerns "total cultural breakdown." Blacks and whites alike are in flight from "denied realities" (p. 464). Valerian Street escapes American seaboard culture and turns his back on the public responsibilities of business and the private ones implicit in being a husband and father. Margaret denies her reality as a mother. Jadine has fled Paris and the truths of her blackness, and even Son, the novel's wild, "natural" man, finally flees Jadine and his American blackness and retreats to the hinterlands of the Caribbean island to join a race of mythic, blind descendants of the slaves who first populated the area.

The author's resolving dense, realistic, social problems with confused and abstract symbolism denotes to readers her own unwillingness to think through the issues clearly.

*   Lange, Bonnie Shipman. "Toni Morrison's Rainbow Code." *Crit.* Cited above as item 69.

186.   Lardner, Susan. "Books: Unastonished Eye." *NY* 57 (June 15, 1981): 147-51.

Throughout her 11 year career which has produced four novels, TM has always created "unsettling" fiction. *TBE* jars readers with its radical contrast between idealized life as presented in primary school readers and the brutal existence led by poor, black Pecola Breedlove. Pecola's pathetic family situation and her consequent withdrawal into insanity are surely startling, but no more so than the varied points of view TM uses in this richly impressionistic little novel.

TB shows the author again experimenting with her unique variety of narrative omniscience that allows expression of personal opinion as well as divergent attitudes "...for which she is not exactly responsible" (p.147). Frequent, imaginative allusions to characters' eyes in each of her works suggest the writer's interest in "disembodied seeing" (p.148) that is simultaneously detached and also implicitly full of fervent involvement.

That tension between authorial feeling on one hand and judgment on the other is at the thematic center of *Sula* in the nurturing and killing behavior of Eva Peace toward her children, as well as in Sula's involvement with Ajax. The book is about love, and the author's judgmental, "dim view" of the emotion is again and again set against her passionately presented feelings regarding the poignancy of such human attachment.

In *SOS,* TM maintains her characteristic authorial ambivalence and her "essential pessimism," (p.149) but she manages to do so while creating a story in which all the ingredients of tragedy are overcome and her male hero--and gender may explain the affirmative difference-- is made capable of exhilarating flight, i.e., regenerative self-discovery.

Now most recently, *TB* extends TM's established pattern of a lush, even exotic style set against grim content. Unfortunately this book is "heavy-handed ...ultimately unintelligible" (p.150), because lacking the coherence of earlier works. Symptomatic of her failure is the title of the book and the opaque metaphor of the tar baby in it. The symbolic function of the tar baby "oversimplifies" and "mak/es/ nonsense of" the highly complicated cultural conflicts the novel attempts to present (p.150). TM's customary gift for vivid, appropriate metaphors deserts her in TB and the overwrought style she adopts deteriorates into bombast (p. 151).

187.   Lyndon, Susan. "What's An Intelligent Woman To Do?" VV (July 1-7, 1981): 40-41.
        For TM, plot is nothing but underpinning for the fabulous allegory she creates. Her means of creation is incredibly lyrical language, a style capable of totally sweeping aside the reader's inclination to disbelieve. In TB her subject is tension: between master and servant, men and women, blacks and whites, and a deep generational tension between younger and older blacks.
        Jadine Childs, a beautiful, cultured, successful black model in Paris, is from the beginning of the book deeply confused about who and what she wants to be. After experiencing an eye opening incident with another self-confident black woman in the supermarket, Jadine returns from Paris to her home in the Caribbean where her aunt and uncle are cook and butler respectively to a wealthy, acutely unhappy white couple, Valerian and Margaret Street. Their ostensibly idyllic, insular lives are interrupted by the forceful intrusion of a black ex-convict named Son, whose physical and psychological presence provokes an unsettling revelation from the Streets' past.
        For Jadine, the problems raised by Son are both sexual and racial. He despises her assimilation into white culture and taunts her with the image of her becoming a "mammy" for the rest of her life if indeed she does what she intends and marries a wealthy Parisian lover. Yet she is just as fearful of being broken by a man such as Son, to whom she is passionately drawn. Being a mammy to his children threatens the social and professional advances she has made too, so finally she flees him, a desperation move. Son pursues her back to the island, but there is told by Therese, a blind oracular character descended from the island's original slave settlers, to forget Jadine, because she "has forgotten her ancient properties" (p. 41).
        Both racism and sexism, which are here presented as being analagous and implicitly violent, have trapped Jadine. She is neither black nor white. She cannot serve white wealth as do her uncle Sydney and aunt Ondine, nor can she abide the militancy of Son. She is tormented by dreams of women offering their breasts to her, yet overwhelmed by the conviction that she can't compete with the "statewide pussy" who was Son's wife, a woman he killed in a rage, in fact. Michael, the mysterious son who is the object of a nasty truth about Margaret Street, has in the past urged Jadine to be a thoughtful, politically conscious individual, but for her there is no workable version of that ideology.

The insidious antagonist to female freedom in *TB* is not society's external limitations, but internal limits imposed by women on themselves. The very realization of their power promotes in women a fear of being successful. Jadine has been trained by society in the same way men have been; in many ways she thinks and believes with the freedom which men have always assumed for themselves. But placed in an either-or situation, Jadine fears to live with the assertiveness of a man. To accept Son's love for her, which is adoring and respectful but also demanding, Jadine would have to lose the self which she has become.

Whether the tar baby of the title is Jadine, or Son, or the woman in the supermarket remains a mystery, just as this author herself is a mystery of femaleness and power, and as her prose is mysterious and vital. Jadine, the pathetic protagonist of the book, is neither "female enough" nor "black enough, culturally speaking," to be a figure of either mystery or power.

188. Moorehead, Caroline. "The New Alan Paton." *Spec* 247 (December 19, 1981): 33.

The most important character in the novel is Valerian and Margaret Street's son, Michael, who never appears. His absence, and the intrusion in the insulated Caribbean atmosphere of a wanted man appropriately named "Son," discloses a welter "of racial hatred and remembered bitterness" in the assembled characters (p. 33). Jadine and Son temporarily leave the island, where they have made themselves believe they are happy with each other, for New York City and Florida, but return to submerge themselves in its superstitions and myths. A character can be "both an individual and a model of their race and history..." (p. 33) in this work whose language is exotic without slipping over into being absurd.

189. O'Meally, Robert G. "'Tar Baby, She Don' Say Nothin.'" *Callaloo* 4 (October-February, 1981): 193-98.

TB received all the hype Madison Avenue could muster: advance copies in bookstores, trade and leather bound special editions, expansive reviews in key publications, interviews with the author (who made the cover of *Newsweek)* on radio and television, book parties--the works. Result: it rapidly sold out of six editions.

That kind of media blitz tends to blur one's judgement, but the work--though structurally intricate and full of impressive images--lacks the "spark of life" that might raise it from formula fiction to "vibrant art" (p. 193).

TB is a novel about blackness, what that is and what "it ain't" (p.194). That theme is dramatized by the confrontation between Jadine (Jade) Childs and William (Son) Green as they search for a home in this world where they can be comfortable with each other and at peace with their community. Jade prefers New York City ("if ever there was a black woman's town, New York City was it," p.195). Son argues for the rural virtues of down-home life in Eloe, Florida, where he believes Jadine can rediscover the "ancient properties" of being a woman, a daughter, a parent, that she has forgotten by virtue of assimilation into white culture.

Most distinctive is TM's reshaping of the tar baby folk story, which effectively condenses the main features of "the blackness of blackness" theme. Jadine is one type of tar baby ("the 'she' of the tales who don' say nothin,' " p.196) who threatens to entrap Son. So too is the African woman in Paris who mocks Jadine's supposed success a type of tar baby: "a black woman ... with skin like tar, with elements strong enough to hold not only one man but a people's tradition" (p. 197). And Son himself is a tar baby-trickster, storyteller, "wanderer hoping to capture the world traveler and take her home to blackness" (p. 197).

The multiple subjects TM's novel conjures up from the complex tar baby material might well pertain to people of many races, but finally her characters do not truly animate the themes. As a result, *TB* appeals essentially to mind, not to the heart, and is less artistically successful than *Sula* or *SOS*.

190.   Pinckney, Darryl. "Every-Which Way." *NYRB*   30 April, 1981, pp. 24-25.

TM's first three novels represent a related "body" of work, bound together by similar settings and themes and a folksy tone which both united the black people in her various real and imagined fictional communities, and at the same time opened up their lives for readers.

In *TB* Morrison changes all her strategies. She locates the action on an imagined Caribbean island, Isle des Chevaliers, off Dominique. And she wraps the origins of communal life there in a haunting fisherman's tale about slaves escaping a sinking French ship, blinded upon seeing Dominique for the first time, but surviving with their horses to occupy the land. Their descendants, the story goes, still control the island's forests and swamps.

Besides radically altering locale, TM here creates a different economic context for looking at race and gender problems. *TB* relates enduring concerns to a generally wealthy, leisured class; hence fashion, commodities, the experiences of the privileged--these function prominently in the narration. Still, the fictional world presented is recognizable to readers as "oppressively parochial and provincial" (24).

The white, ostensibly "master" couple live empty indolent lives. Valerian Street divides his time between his greenhouse, where he pampers his plants with verbal petting and music, and his dining room, where he alternaltely mocks, accuses, and otherwise tortures his wife Margaret. Like many couples, Valerian and Margaret share little other than the same cage.

Sydney and Ondine, black butler and cook for the Streets for years, have been seriously discomfitted by the move from New England which threatens their supposedly golden years. Their hope for the last part of their lives is a Sorbonne-educated, high fashion model, their niece Jadine. Despite access to all the so-called advantages of western culture, Jadine has none of the tensile strength or self-reliance of TM's earlier women characters. She is herself ambivalent about the value of black culture and her own identity as a black woman. In her private moments, she reflectively admits to being disinterested in some of the cosmetic aspects of her heritage such as distinctive jewelry, and to being quite unmoved by the acknowledged masters of black music, in particular jazz. She yearns in an elemental, basic way "to get out of /her/ skin and be only the person inside..." (p. 24).

Christmas at the mansion brings not the return of the much discussed, prodigal son Michael, but a black ex-convict whose values clash resoundingly with everyone's, and whose presence provokes the novel's debate on gender, culture, and personal morality. As the lives of the four older characters unravel, the disintegration sparked by the revelation of a grim truth out of Valerian and Margaret's past, Jade and Son leave in search of a meaningful life for themselves.

They cannot find it. Neither can accommodate the basic values of the other. Son despises her New York City as much as she is repulsed by the backwardness of his rural Florida. After much violent fighting and reconciling, Jadine leaves Son for life "in the fast lane in Paris" (p. 25). He pursues her as far as the Isle des Chevaliers, where he disappears into the swamp to join the legendary slave settlers. Though he concedes the ambiguity of the book's closing, Pinckney assumes that what Son is going to "is no good, desperate" (p. 25).

This critic's dissatisfaction with the book fixes on its elaborate, distracting, and obscure prose--usually found in descriptive passages. He does not believe TM's personifying of nature is either interesting or effective, and more importantly, even the feelings of the characters occasionally become indecipherable because the narrative conveys character thoughts in the same way: by imposing human qualities on inanimate objects.

Admittedly the aim of *TB* is to generate an atmosphere of myth and mystery such as is found impressively present in the fiction of Carpentier, Asturias, and Marquez. But what is accomplished is far less than what was attempted, and the language of *TB* "is, at best, strained, and the convoluted verbal conjurings make for a tone that is overreaching, taxing..." (p. 25).

An uncertainty in conception and an ambiguity in execution make even the symbolic figure of the title unnecessarily puzzling to readers. In anthropological terms (cf. the work of Melville

Herskovits), the tar baby is certainly not benevolent. It is "a monster who stalks the woods near plantations, preying on children." In folklore, he is more genial and amusing, "a trickster thief who gets trapped in his own snare" (p. 25). Pinckney is not able to sort out the discrepancy, so settles for saying both readings could be applicable to TM's book.

The urgency manifest in recent fiction by Afro-American women (focused on domestic violence, conjugal brutality) is noticeably missing from *TB*. To suggest what might have been, the critic closes by alluding to the unsentimental language of Gayl Jones and wishing TM's book were different from what in fact it is.

191.   Reyes, Angelita D. "Crossing The Bridge: The Great Mother in Selected Novels of Toni Morrison, Paule Marshall, Simone Schwarz-Bart, and Mariama Ba." Ph.D. diss., University of Iowa. *DAI*. 46 (1985): 1618-A.

The archetype of the Great Mother is viably present in four novels by contemporary black women and it is here the basis of a cross-cultural literary analysis. Using theoretical concepts of Mircea Eliade, Victor Turner, Isidore Okpewho, and Erich Neumann, that archetype is examined in Africa and the New World in order to establish its range and attributes. In the case of TM, the fact that the central character of *TB* (Jadine Childs) lacks the qualities of the archetype implies that according to this novel such a presence is necessary to hold black culture together.

192.   Rodman, Selden. "Whites and Blacks." *NRev* 33 (June 26, 1981): 730-32.

Reading (and reviewing) fiction about relations between blacks and whites is a task which seems to presume the presence of a bias one way or the other. TM's treatment of characters is less than even-handed in *TB* but reviewers thus far have tacitly approved of her slanted view, or else have been embarrassed to raise the point. Rodman argues the novel is "thinly disguised Black Power propaganda" (p. 731).

The fact that the author consistently capitalizes Black and uses lower case for white signals her flagrant bias in favor of the one group and condescension toward the other. Valerian Street is lashed in the prose for every aspect of his "capitalist-imperialist-sexist" (p. 731) life style, his wife Margaret disclosed as a closet racist and child abuser. Even the Caribbean island setting is romanticized, and its establishing details are, in significant instances, factually inaccurate.

Lacking subtlety as it does, *TB* makes its moral patently obvious: whites and blacks can work together, but cannot share in any of the "personal things in life" (p.732).

193.   Rumens, Carol. "Conflicts of Complexion." *TLS* 30 October, 1981, p.1260.
TM polarizes the issue of racial conflict in *TB* by focusing the reader's attention not on material things but on "unresolved conflicts within and between /the/ brilliantly differentiated personalities" (p. 1260) of her small cast of representative characters. Principal among them are Margaret Street, an outcast in her monied, white society, and Jadine Childs, a highly educated and less-than-black niece of the Streets' black servants. Jadine's appearance of having "made it" in white European culture is belied by a recurring nightmare in which maternal black women menace her. Self-doubt is further heightened by her passionate affair with the black fugitive, Son, who taunts Jadine with being the tar baby trap of folklore created by the white farmer.

Ultimately we do not know for sure whether Son chooses his passion for Jadine or "the racial integrity" (p.1260) symbolized by the ghosts of wild, blind horsemen descended from slaves and said to inhabit the island's mountains.

To read this writer's prose with understanding, one must be alert to symbolical and metaphorical meaning embedded in her allusive language, because she frequently personifies the clouds, trees, river, and hills of the natural setting.

194.   Schott, Webster. "Toni Morrison: Tearing The Social Fabric." *Book World* 22 March, 1981, pp. 1-2.
Choosing to be confrontive, TM hits her readers with a novel of ideas that challenges customary notions of love, of racial integration, and even of the wisdom of seeking happiness by living "accommodated" lives.

Place is essential in her fiction, because settings force human responses,and those responses reveal character. Into the Caribbean island setting she draws as being rife with examples of economic and emotional bondage comes a truly free black man. Son Green is TM's heroic male, yearning for "his sources, not a future of assimilation" (p. 1).

Within a short time Son has outraged the inhabitants of the house he invades, upset every semblance of normal order, and caused the haughty Jadine to fall passionately in love. Once having rattled Valerian Street's sense of authority and forced the revelation of Margaret's abuse of her son Michael, Son leaves the island with Jadine, intending to show her what "real life" is like in his home of Eloe, Florida. For her that place is a potential prison, no Eden. She feels oppressed by the conservative sexual values as those apply to women, and abandons Son for her Parisian lover. The heroic Son returns to nature on the Isle des Chevaliers.

TM's racial ideas are assertively hostile: "that blacks seek ways to hate whites, that black people cannot be fully human on white values, that integration is another way of control, that physical prowess is embedded in black masculinity" (p. 2). What finally keeps the work from being completely successful is an absence of adequate internal motivation for what the characters do. Thus accepting them as characters does not lead to one's believing in their behavior, which seems to have been imposed on them by the author. Such is often the fate of novels of ideas.

195.   Sheed, Wilfrid. "Improbable Assignment: *Tar Baby*." *Atl* 247 (April, 1981): 119-20.
TM's command of the "secrets" of the black, group experience is complete. Her knowledge of such central truths provides her a subject, while her sensitivity to the nuances of language affords her a variety of "sounds:" mirthful (cf. Pearl Bailey), sly (cf. Billie Holiday), and deep (cf. Ethel Waters).
If *TB* is her weakest work to date, that is because she has tried to do too much in cramming her expansive themes into "a comedy of manners" (p.119). *TBE* and *Sula* played relatively simple motifs ("one-to-two-note books"), but *TB* is complicated, diverse, and many layered like *SOS*. TM appears to have set out to fashion a play with Valerian Street's greenhouse as the set and his urbane malaise played against Margaret's scatterbrained-mother-waiting-for-prodigal-son's-return-for-Christmas. Then their carefully maintained deceptions are destroyed by the arrival of the black drifter, Son, who agitates them into painful self-analysis (the rising action of Act 11) and rudely jolts Jadine from her torpid existence on the edge of high fashion, western culture and an interracial marriage. Jadine's and Son's affair provokes a clash with no middle ground. By themselves, they are capable of realizing edenic passion; with other people--whether in her world or his--they are tragically displaced.
The author's judgmental presence broods over the book (suggesting the distinct possibility of its being autobiographical), and yet its conclusion "is irresolute, almost a 'Lady and the Tiger' affair" (p. 120) that is quite unsatisfying. The hollowness apparent is the result of the disjunction between a novel that is complete and an ending that is not finished.

196.   Sheppard, R.Z. "Black Diamond: *Tar Baby*." *Time* 117 (March 16, 1981): 90-92.
Drawing upon the Caribbean and its "buried history of slavetrade and uprisings" and its evocative atmosphere of "negritude," (p. 92) TM spins a story of characters with their emotions held carefully in check. Valerian and Margaret Street maintain distanced lives together, and their employees, Sydney and Ondine, brood over

their own sour secrets. Precarious emotional equilibriums are unbalanced by the intrusion of a ragged black man fleeing a charge of wife-murder in Florida. Particularly unnerved is Sydney's niece, Jadine, who must eventually choose between a sophisticated French lover and the intruder, Son Green, a "black diamond in the rough" (p. 91).

Racial and cultural conflicts erupt for Jadine and Son, along with psychological tensions associated with child abuse in the mother figures Margaret and Ondine. All the complications are presented in "a ripe, sometimes overripe, prose style" (p. 92) consistent with the atmosphere of magical realism that pervades the novel, yet ultimately the book "does not quite work" (p. 92).

197.   Shrimpton, Nicholas. "Well jointed & highly polished." *NS* 102 (October 23, 1981): 22.

TM is of course a member of the black minority in America, but still there is something identifiably mainstream about her fourth novel. The reviewer cites it as an instance of "high-falutin'" American fiction, the type which tends to be marked by poetic language and a "punchy plot" that stirs together "child-battering, ecology, blacks and women" (p. 22). The story of Jadine Childs' love for a man whose character epitomizes the black culture she is-- with years of effort and at great expense--escaping, forces her to choose between the values of Europe and "the claims of her genetic heritage" (p. 22). Issues which the author has selected to consider are topical and indeed significant, but as handled in this "thin" book, they become "seriously overweight" (p. 22).

198.   Smith, Valerie. "Remembering One's Ancient Properties: *Tar Baby* ." *SewRev* 89 (October, 1981): cxv.

The "tar baby" of this novel is "Son" Green, a black fugitive who invades the physical and psychological complacency of Valerian and Margaret Street's Caribbean island retreat and who, with his shocking presence, "touches" all the assembled characters at their deepest emotional levels. Valerian's carefully cultivated graciousness, Margaret's pose as the anxious mother longing for her son's return, Ondine's mask of courtesy to her employer's wife, Jadine's sense of satisfaction in western cosmopolitan values--all such surfaces are stripped away revealing the awful, sticky truths at the characters' centers. As was the case in *SOS*, the action of *TB* forces characters to come to terms with their history--as women, as men, as parents, as blacks, and as white.

This is TM's most ambitious book, even though it is occasionally flawed by inappropriate imagery applied to local history and landscapes (p.cxvii).

199. Spigner, Nieda. "A 'Best' Seller." *Freedomways* 21 (1981): 267-69.
Uncle Remus' story of the tar baby here functions as the major premise of a new best seller by TM. In her reworking of the folk material, TM suggests the tar baby is a black woman shaped by a white man in order to entrap a black man.

On a lush Caribbean island, millionaire Valerian Street educates and cultivates the beautiful niece of his black servants. Her allure as the "new black woman" (strong, independent, sexy but not nurturing) captivates "Son," the black male intruder whose provocative presence strips away all bourgeoise pretensions from the Streets and their aging, security conscious servants. Jadine is elegant, Son crude. Neither can be at home in the other's world, they discover as a consequence of disappointing visits to both, and in the end they part without "having gained wisdom or insight into one another's dilemma" (p. 268).

One cannot be sure of TM's intention for her characters, who seem believable only in their highly artificial setting. What is certain is the author's firm grasp of what is required to make a novel marketable.

* Strous, Jean. "Toni Morrison's Black Magic." *Newsweek*. Cited above as item 54.

200. "Tar Baby." *KR* 49 (January 1, 1981): 33.
"Fine-tuned" characters both black and white meet on a Caribbean island, the atmosphere of which is thick with mythic and animistic fancies. At Christmas dinner their delicately balanced relationships (illustrative of the variety of "dependences" TM examines in the book as a whole) come apart because of revealing confrontations about the past. Jade and Son flee to New York City, but find they have no real life together, despite having come to believe that is the only life either of them would wish. She is "successful" only in a commercial sense as the book closes, and Son drops back into a "ghostly" past. Despite its mythic context, the novel is highlighted by "scouring" contemporary insights (p. 33).

201. "Tar Baby." *VQR* 57 (Autumn, 1981): 135.
TB is the "most ambitious" of TM's novels, addressing as it does the major concerns of all three earlier works. In addition to probing the conflicts between black women and men, this book gives readers TM's "first fully fleshed ... white characters" (p. 135).

Jadine Childs and Son, the black renegade to whom she is intensely drawn, are the tar baby and rabbit of black folklore. Their excessive dialogue is one weakness in the work, a second is a "too frequent use of the pathetic fallacy" (p.135) that detracts from the author's lush style.

202.   Winslow, Henry F., Sr. "Book Corner: *Tar Baby.*" *Crisis* 88 (June, 1981): 247-48.

TB, the fourth novel by the "literary mother figure among modern fiction's major writers" (p. 247), is a kind of extension of the theme of Fannie Hurst's *Imitation of Life* (1933). Both examine the values, the fears, and frustrations of a light-complexioned black woman. Jadine's opposite is "Son" Green, a "natural" black man who gets under her skin and provokes her to reconsider her lifestyle and learned values. He also prompts painful and risky self-examination in her aunt and uncle, an older black couple whose cultural energy has been consumed in a lifetime of domestic service, as well as in the "superior," wealthy whites who literally own the entire "stage on which Miss Morrison's comic romance is acted out" (p. 247).

Impressively real, engaging characters occupy the stage, and the integrity with which TM treats sensitive racial and cultural themes distinguish her from contemporaries (Irwin Shaw, Marilyn French, Judith Krantz) whose work has been promoted into prominence. TM's fiction needs to be known by all literate Americans.

PART VI
AWARDS AND HONORS

SONG OF
SOLOMON

A NOVEL BY
Toni
Morrison

203. Book of The Month Club alternate selection, *Sula* 1975.

204. National Book Award nomination for *Sula,* 1975.

205. American Academy and Institute of Arts and Letters Award for *Song of Solomon,* 1977.

206. Book of The Month Club main selection, *Song of Solomon,* 1977.

207. National Book Critics Circle Award for *Song of Solomon,* 1977.

208. Distinguished Writer of 1978, American Academy of Arts and Letters.

209. Cleveland Arts Prize in Literature, 1978.

210. National Council On The Arts, 1980 appointment by President Jimmie Carter.

211. Elected to the American Academy And Institute Of Arts And Letters, 1981.

212. New York State Governor's Arts Award, 1986.

213. City College of New York Langston Hughes Festival Award (Medallion), 1986.

214. Washington College Literary Award, 1987.

215. Book of The Month Club main selection, *Beloved,* 1987.

216. Doctor of Letters, *honoris causa*, granted by the College of Saint Rose, Albany, New York, March , 1987.

217.   Baraka, Amiri and Amina Baraka, editors. *Confirmation: An Anthology of African-American Women.* New York: Quill, 1983. Includes "Recitatif."

  *   Bonetti, Kay. "Toni Morrison Interview." *American Audio Prose Library*, Columbia, Mo. May, 1983, 78 minutes. Cited above as item 28.

218.   Harper, Michael S. and Robert B. Stepto, editors. *Chant of Saints, A Gathering of Afro-American Literature, Art, and Scholarship.* Chicago and London: University of Illinois Press, 1979. Includes "Intimate Things in Place: A Conversation with Toni Morrison," and an excerpt from *Sula.*

219.   Morrison, Toni. "Reading From *Tar Baby*." *American Audio Prose Library*, Columbia, MO. 55 minutes. Following a brief introduction by the AAPL host which sketches biographical features about TM, the author reads three sections from *TB*, beginning with an excerpt from Chapter 2 which describes Jadine's shocking encounter with the haughtily self-assured African woman. Next is a lengthy selection from Chapter 8, the description and analysis of Valerian Street and Margaret as they reflect on her abuse of their son. Finally, TM includes a part of Chapter 5, p. 165, a delineation of the character of the "undocumented man," Son Green.

220.   Morrison, Toni. "Song of Solomon." *Random House Audio Books*. New York: Alfred A. Knopf, Inc., 1977. 2 hours 58 minutes. This presentation is an abridgement which aims to give the listener a sense of the whole novel. Morrison's reading of sequential excerpts from nearly every chapter are strung together by narrator William Fowler's summaries of material omitted.

221.   Troupe, Quincy and Rainer Schulte, compilers and editors. *Giant Talk: An Anthology of Third World Writing.* New York: Random House, 1975. Includes "1923," an excerpt from *Sula.*

222.   Washington, Mary Helen, editor. *Black-Eyed Susans, Classic Stories By and About Black Women.* New York: Anchor Press, Doubleday, 1975.

Includes "The Coming of Maureen Peal," and "SEEMOTHERMOTHERISVERYNICE," excerpts from *The Bluest Eye.*

223. Washington, Mary Helen, editor. *Midnight Birds, Stories of Contemporary Black Women Writers.* New York: Anchor Press, Doubleday, 1980.
      Includes "Eva Peace," an excerpt from *Sula.*

PART VIII
RELATED REFERENCES

224.   Begnal, Kate. "Toni Morrison." in *Critical Survey of Long Fiction*.
        Edited by Frank MacGill. Englewood Cliffs, NJ: Salem Press, 1983.
        Vol. 5.

225.   *Book Revew Digest*. New York: H.W. Wilson Company, 1970-
        1985.

226.   Davis, Marianna W., editor. *Contributions of Black Women to
        America, International Dictionary of Women's Biography*. Columbia,
        S.C.: Kenday Press, 1981, 1982.

227.   Davis, Thadious M., and Trudier Harris, editors. *Dictionary of
        Literary Biography, Afro-American Writers After 1955*. Detroit: Gale
        Research Company, 1984. Vol. 33.

228.   deVaux, Paula, editor. *Current Book Review Citations*. New York:
        The Wilson Company, 1976-1982.

229.   Evory, Ann, editor. *Contemporary Authors,* New Revision Series.
        Detroit: Gale Research Company, 1972, 1978. Vols. 29-32.

230.   Fairbanks, Carol and Eugene A. Engeldinger, editors. *Black
        American Fiction, A Bibliography*. Metuchen, New Jersey and
        London: Scarecrow Press, 1978.

231.   Fikes, Robert, Jr. "Echoes From Small Town Ohio: A Toni
        Morrison Bibliography." *Obsidian* 5, i-ii (1979): 142-48.

232.   Houston, Helen R. *The Afro-American Novel, 1865-1975: A
        Descriptive Bibliography of Primary and Secondary Sources*. Troy,
        NY: Whitston Publishing, 1977.

233.   Kibler, James E. Jr., editor. *Dictionary of Literary Biography:
        American Novelists Since World War II*. Second Series. Detroit:
        Gale Research Company, 1980. Vol. 6.

170

234.   Lee, A. Robert, editor. *Black Fiction, New Studies in the Afro-American Novel Since 1945*. New York: Barnes and Noble, 1980.

235.   Magill, Frank, editor. *Magill's Bibliography of Literary Criticism*. Englewood Cliffs, NJ: Salem Press, 1979. 3 volumes, vol.3.

236.   Margolies, Edward and David Bakish, editors. *Afro-American Fiction, 1853-1976, A Guide To Information Sources*. Detroit: Gale Research Company, 1979.

237.   Page, James A. and Jae Min Roh, editors. *Selected Black American, African, and Caribbean Authors, a Bio-Bibliography*. Littleton, Colorado: Libraries Unlimited, 1985.

238.   Rood, Karen L., Jean W. Ross, and Richard Ziegfeld, editors. *Dictionary of Literary Biography Yearbook: 1981*. Detroit: Gale Research Company, 1982.

239.   Rosenblatt, Roger. *Black Fiction*. Cambridge, MA and London: Harvard University Press, 1974.

240.   Rush, Theressa Gunnels, Carol Fairbanks Myers, and Esther Spring Arata, editors. *Black American Writers Past and Present: A Biographical and Bibliographical Dictionary*. Metuchen, NJ: Scarecrow Press, 1975. Vol. 2.

241.   Stine, Jean C. *Contemporary Literary Criticism*. Detroit: Gale Research Company, 1984. 28 volumes. Vol. 4, 10, 22.

242.   Tarbert, Gary C., editor. *Book Review Index*. Detroit: Gale Research Company, 1965-1985.

243.   Wasserman, Steven R., editor. *The Lively Arts Information Directory: A Guide To the Fields of Music, Dance, Theatre, Film, Radio, and Television, For the United States and Canda*. Detroit: Gale Research Company, 1982.

244.   Whitlaw, Roger. *Black American Literature, A Critical History*. Chicago: Nelson-Hall Company, 1973.

PART IX
MEMBERSHIPS

245.   Advisory Board, New York African American Institute, SUNY.

246.   Board of Trustees, New York Public Library.

247.   Council Member, Author's Guild.

248.   Dramatist's Guild of America.

249.   Helsinki Watch Committee.

250.   Member, American Academy of Arts & Letters.

251.   Member, Queens College Corporate Advisory Board.

252.   National Advisory Board, Center for the Study of Southern Culture.

253.   National Council on the Arts,

254.   Officer, Author's League.

255.   Writer's Guild of America.

PART X
INDEX

POSTSCRIPT

Beloved. New York: Knopf, 1987.

This book appeared too late to be considered in detail here. The following items are cited as evidence of the high praise and muted criticism the new novel appears bound to receive.

Atwood, Margaret. "Haunted By Their Nightmares: *Beloved.*" *NYTBR* 13 September, 1987, pp. 1, 49-50.

Beloved is a hair-raising read, an inspired work of fiction, successful in both technical and emotional terms, certain to confirm TM's stature among pre-eminent American novelists.

The novel concerns both the era of slavery in the U.S. and the Reconstruction which followed. It is set partly in Cincinnati, where the freed slaves who dominate the story now struggle with emotional bondage, and it is set partly in Kentucky at the plantation where their history was focused in the miserable past.

Beloved is a ghost story, but an original of the type. Sethe, its protagonist, lives immersed in grief and guilt as a consequence of having killed her two year old daughter 18 years before. Sethe's "choice," like that of the equally entrapped Sophie, is between repugnant alternatives and is forced upon her by an inhuman system. The literal result of her decision is that the "sad, malicious" ghost of the slain child now resides with Sethe and Denver, her surviving daughter, and threatens to ruin their lives. Ironically, Sethe would rather have the ghost of her Beloved child with her than nothing at all. Hers is a fractured family, yet it is better than most had under the tyranny of slavery. TM's dramatization of the slave past reveals it as a "viciously antifamily institution/ /" (p. 49) with the express aim of obliterating all relationships and any sense of community.

Hard though she is on the white characters in the book, TM is aware of the need to balance her total picture. Her black characters are not all wonderful either. The neighborhood around Sethe indulges in scapegoating (as was true in *Sula*), and the black males have decided "limitations and flaws" (as was true in both *Sula* and *SOS*). Folklore remains a major preoccupation with TM, particularly folklore concerning the dead. Also, her prose retains its "antiminimalist" quality as she works to evoke a sort of magic atmosphere through the use of alternately lush and lyrical then homely and colloquial styles.

Hinted at by the epigraph to the book (from Romans 9: 25) is the message that acceptance is now forthcoming for those formerly considered despised outsiders.

Smith, Amanda. "Toni Morrison." *Publisher's Weekly* 21 August, 1987, pp. 50-51.

This interview, done a month before the publication of *Beloved,* locates the source of TM's fifth novel in a story the author discovered while editing *TBB*. (The slave woman who ran away and who, when captured, tried to kill her children became for Morrison a haunting model of human dignity, of the universal and overwhelming hunger for love, and of the anguish, the intimacy, the joy of being a woman.) This black woman insisted upon the sovereignty of her personhood even when faced by a system that claimed to own her; she became a representative of all "those black slaves whom we don't know. . . who amounted to a nation who simply left one place, disappeared and didn't show up on the other shores" (p. 51). Those folk comprise the gone-community, "the disremembered and unaccounted for" in this novel about the need to be free of slavery.

TM's own enriching childhood, spent in the midst of a supportive (sometimes intrusively so) community that subtly molded many of her adult values is discussed in the interview as an informing context for this latest work.

Perhaps with a glance backward at critical evaluations of her characterization in previous novels as being "exaggerated," and then anticipating similar scolding for having used a ghost as a flesh and blood figure in *Beloved,* TM observes wryly that her fictional folks are only "as big as life, not bigger than." But she adds a comment which makes clear the breadth of her artistic vision and asserts that it is she, not her detractors, who sees things truly: "Life is very big. . . . If some of my characters are as big as the life they have, they may seem enormous exaggerations, but /only to/ a reader whose sense of life is more diminished than mine" (p. 51).

Snitow, Ann. "Death Duties, Toni Morrison Looks Back in Sorrow." *VV, Literary Supplement* 8 September, 1987, pp. 25-26.

Like other examples of holocaust writing, *Beloved* is a novel of terror, of devastating personal and cultural loss, of exorcism of the past urgently necessary so as to be capable of moving forward with life. It is also a book that insists the countless "disremembered and unaccounted for" whose lives are erased by the grinding of such history must not be forgotten.

As in both *SOS* and *TB*, Morrison structures her fiction around the supernatural. Beset by the ghost of her slain two year old baby, Sethe and her other daughter, Denver, are in 1873 survivors of slavery continuing to struggle against its numbing aftereffects and against their extended grief which has become palpably real. The ghost called Beloved, whether known by the puckish tricks she plays or as a fearsome female come back to seduce the otherwise sensible Paul D and further subjugate Sethe and Denver, is the central figure of the book. Beloved is "a projection of Sethe's longing. . . . a snare to catch her anguished . . . mother's heart" (p. 25). Though Sethe suffers terribly while a slave and thereafter, her "inner life miraculously expands beyond the narrow law of cause and effect" (p. 26) to afford her happiness in the end. Yearn though we may for such a conclusion to this narrative of horrific hurt, when it is given to us, that upbeat resolution seems contrived.

Finally, assessment of the book must focus on the ghost of Beloved. Considered simply in technical terms, TM's use of that strategy does bring to life the slave experience and thus it "makes thematic sense" (p. 26). Radical indeed is TM's aim to craft a memorable, affirmative novel from the story of a "slave baby murdered by its own mother" (p. 26). But the ghost is also a strained device; it does not provide a viable psychic center for the book because the demon female remains disturbingly static throughout. This is a character who, instead of enriching the fiction, distracts the reader (and the writer) from the living characters.

TM is always an ambitious author. She aims to communicate the spiritual complexity of black tradition with beautiful prose, and with memorable characters and dialogue fused together in a grandly romantic vision that inspires and heals. If her fiction splinters the human experience as we see it in *Beloved,* still the fiction does not become the "fragmented narrative of modernism" (p. 26). If the book is "hollow in the middle," it certainly does not lack integrity. TM has simply not in this instance discovered the form that will adequately embody her rich, poetic vision as she did in *Sula*, her most successful fusion to date of supernatural content and credibly real vehicle.